April 11, 2022

ⓒ 2019

LAKE CHAPALA

BENEATH THE SURFACE

CONSIDERATIONS FOR RETIRING IN MEXICO

By Bill Dahl

Lake Chapala
Beneath The Surface

Bill Dahl

3

COPYRIGHT © 2019 BY WILLIAM S. DAHL

Library of Congress Cataloging-in-Publication Data

Dahl, William S., 1954-

Lake Chapala – Beneath The Surface - Considerations for Retiring in Mexico

Pages 155 cm.

Includes bibliographical references, index and notes.

Library of Congress Catalogue Number:

ISBN: 13: 978-0-9835836-2-2

1. Lake Chapala 2. Mexico 3. Retirement in Mexico 4. Environmental and Public Health Hazards 5. Corruption

TABLE OF CONTENTS

ACKNOWLEDGMENTS

To THE Most Precious Gift in life, my wife,

Jacqueline J. Dahl.

PROLOGUE

This book is the product of considering the possibility of retirement in the Lake Chapala (Ajijic/Lakeside) area of Jalisco Mexico.

You have probably read about this area on-line and the thousands of ex-pats, snow- birds and full time residents from the U.S., Canada and Europe that reside there. It has been a tremendously popular destination primarily for retirees from North America.

After completing extensive on-line research, my wife and I travelled to this area together in August 2018. I returned for another two week visit and a seminar about retiring in Mexico in October/November 2018.

The result is this book. It is a look beneath the surface of the Lake Chapala area that will further inform your considerations for retiring there.

Every place on Earth has its strengths and weaknesses. Chapala, Ajijic, and the other Lakeside communities are no exception. However, local social media groups, blogs and web boards are heavily represented by posts accentuating the positives. This is also true of the social media content displayed via ex-pat blogs, YouTube videos, international living sites (and magazines), real estate companies, international traveler blogs, and sites dedicated to retirement in Mexico. One would not expect anything different from insiders or those who have interests where accentuating the positive is fundamental to their ongoing viability. Many folks considering retirement in the Lake Chapala area limit their research to these social media resources.

During our investigation of the area, there were a few things that inspired me to dig deeper – beneath the surface of Lake Chapala. I never saw anyone swimming in the Lake. I never saw pets in the water. I witnessed Mexican resident fishermen spraying pesticides on the water lilies that inhabit the lake. I never saw anyone recreating on the lake (with the exception of rides in tourist boats departing from the shore of the municipality of Chapala). There were notices in our hotel room declaring "Don't drink the water!"

I am a writer, observer, researcher and photographer by training. These skills inhabit me and are aroused when circumstances evoke the same. Thus, I went beneath the surface to explore this reality. There's a lot more to the proposition of retiring in/around Lake Chapala than meets the eye.

Mexico is not unlike any other country on the planet; it possesses extraordinary positives it is proud to share with the world – and – it has current issues that it would rather not speak about. I encountered both.

It should be stated from the outset that *I adore Mexico -* especially Guadalajara in the State of Jalisco. The people, culture, language, food, art, architecture, history, and landscapes are precious to me. I did not travel to Mexico with this book in mind. The inspirations for this book *found me* – my heart *and* my mind. The motivation for this series was both unexpected and unintentional. Yet, when confronted with these realities, I knew I must write about them.

ENJOY the journey. I certainly did. Expect the unexpected.

That's Mexico.

I hope you enjoy this book. May this work more fully inform your evaluation of the possibility of retiring in the Mexico's Lake Chapala.

Bill Dahl – January 2019

CHAPTER ONE

Mexiconsiderations:

North American Retirees Moving to Mexico

"Where should I retire?" It's a common question in North America as Baby Boomers contemplate how and where they might spend the remainder of this life. For tens of thousands, this question includes destinations outside the U.S. or Canada. Oftentimes, this process involves mulling over Mexico. Every January, the publication *International Living*, provides retirees with suggestions using their Annual Global Retirement Index. In 2018, Mexico was ranked as the 2nd Best Place to retire by *IL*. Estimates vary, but it's safe to conclude that more than a few million Americans and Canadians now reside primarily in Mexico. That's a lot of Gringos who have made the leap.

My wife and I began pondering this question last year. We call this process our Mexiconsiderations. We spent hours upon hours searching the internet, watching a few hundred YouTube videos, and talking to others about this possibility. This included extensive conversations with our Hispanic friends in the U.S. – most of whom have family and friends currently residing in Mexico. During our marriage, we have traveled to Mexico on numerous occasions. Typically, Puerto Vallarta, Cancun, Cozumel, Mexico City, a cruise to Ensenada, and a walk around Tijuana (for a few hours) – like most American and Canadian tourists do. So, we made a decision.

In August 2018, we set out for a region in Mexico we had never explored before: central Mexico – the state of Jalisco. This region was recommended to us by our Hispanic friends and confirmed by our internet research. What motivated us, along with millions of others? We had four: A reduced cost of living, access to more affordable healthcare, a better climate (no cold and snow), and new cultural adventures.

We flew from our home in Oregon to Guadalajara, Mexico (GDL) – a two stop, 2,300 mile flight (about 12 hours door-to-door) on Alaska Airlines. We stayed at a hotel in Zona Centro Historico in downtown Guadalajara for four days ($56 U.S. per night, for a huge room with an outdoor balcony, including breakfast). We found Guadalajara to be a truly magical city – one that most North American tourists never visit. The people, architecture, art, weather, food, value, transportation, history and culture were mesmerizing. We yearned to return.

We departed Guadalajara via UBER for a 45 minute ride to our hotel in Ajijic (*Ah-hee-heek*) for a 7 day stay, on the shores of Lake Chapala – home to a purported 20,000 expats from the U.S., Canada, Europe, and the U.K. Lake Chapala is the largest body of fresh water in Mexico spanning some 48 miles in length and up to 12 miles wide. It has a superb climate averaging 72 degrees F year round. In August, it is winter in the Chapala area. It rains at night (as it does in Guadalajara). Locals refer to the climate as *eternal spring*. The busy season is November through May when snowbirds arrive from the north to enjoy the area.

You simply cannot come away from a stay on the north shore of Lake Chapala indelibly entranced by its multi-dimensional beauty. The flowers and vegetation are explosive in their myriad of colors, forms and scents. The vistas are fantastic. The people, food, landscape, weather, art, culture, options for activity and entertainment, accommodations, and architecture are all hypnotic. We even took a tour of the area with a local realtor (who had relocated here a year earlier from Wisconsin). Our four primary considerations we set out to explore first hand *appeared* to be verified: A reduced cost of living, access to more affordable healthcare, a better climate, and new cultural adventures.

During our stay in Ajijic, we had the opportunity to meet with couples from the U.S. and Canada who were attending a seminar at the hotel we were staying in. It was called *Focus on Mexico – A Learning Adventure*. These couples, like us, were exploring the possibility of retiring to this area of Mexico. To a person, these folks shared that "I cannot imagine retiring in Mexico without attending the FOM experience." We flew back to the U.S. glowing – *we've found it*.

We continued our discussions and my wife returned to work. "I think you should attend the next Focus on Mexico seminar," she said. I registered for the seminar and confirmed my travel plans for two weeks in late October to early November 2018. I studied to improve my Spanish language skills for 5 weeks prior to departure. We also made a list of questions to answer on this second exploration trip. These included:

What are the *actual* housing costs in the Lakeside market at this time? What does access to more affordable healthcare really mean? What are the immigration and customs considerations? Can we bring our pets and vehicles? What does the area around the entirety of the lake look like? What is the reality for access to Wi-Fi, the internet, and satellite television look like? What is the water quality in the lake? What is the state of the local infrastructure (sewer, wastewater treatment, water quality and electricity)? What about the available options for banking/finance/investment and currency conversion? Is local government stable and adequately funded? What does public safety look like?

I'll provide the answers to these, and other *Mexiconsiderations* in the upcoming chapters in this book.

CHAPTER TWO

Mexiconsiderations Part II

Guidance for North American Boomers Contemplating Retirement in Mexico

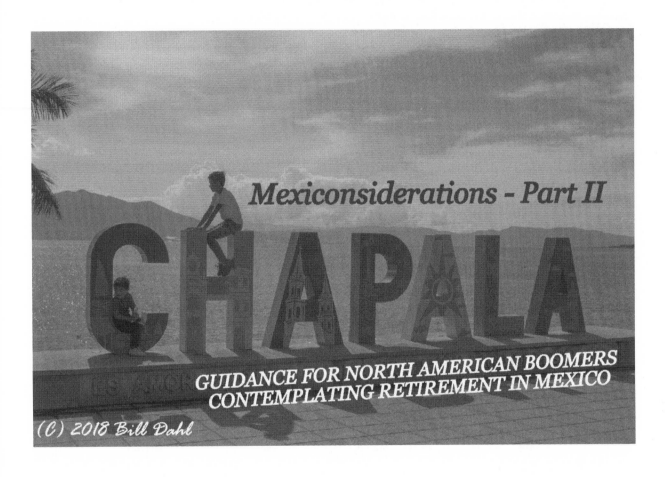

What motivated my wife and me to invest in considering Mexico (*Mexconsiderations*)? We had four: A reduced cost of living, access to more affordable healthcare, a better climate (no cold and snow), and new cultural adventures. We're not alone. According to CBS News, the number of Americans retiring outside the United States is growing exponentially. Between 2010 and 2015 the number grew 17 percent. The figure is expected to rise during the next 10 years as boomer retirement continues.1 According to several sources, Mexico is now considered the preferred retirement home for an estimated 1-2 million American retirees - more than any other country.2

Charles Handy has written: *"The first step is to measure whatever can be easily counted. This is OK as far as it goes. The second step is to disregard that which can't be easily measured or to give it an arbitrary quantitative value. This is artificial and misleading. The third step is to presume that which can't be measured easily really isn't important. This is blindness. The fourth step is to say that which can't be easily measured really doesn't exist. This is suicide.3* For our *Mexiconsiderations*, Handy's quote provides a useful evaluation framework for us. Stay with me.

The First Step - Measure Whatever Can Be Easily Counted:

The weather in the Lake Chapala has been touted as the second best climate on the planet, averaging 72 degrees F year round. At 5,000 feet in elevation, humidity is minimal. During the five month rainy season (June to October) rainfall averages 30 inches annually (mostly during the evenings and at night). The Lake measures some 48 miles in length and 12 miles in width. Towns, villages and cities dot its circumference. It is surrounded by the lush Sierra Madre Mountains. A 40 minute drive from Ajijic-Chapala to the Guadalajara metropolitan area (and Guadalajara International Airport - GDL) is also a plus. Earthquakes occur in this region.1 There are poisonous spiders too. It has been reported that the Guadalajara-Chapala region in Jalisco is the largest retirement community outside the US. 2 The cities of

Chapala and Ajijic are estimated to have resident populations that total 40,000, although estimates vary.3

The 2n Step - Disregard That Which Can't Be Easily Measured or Give it An Arbitrary Quantitative Value:

How many of *us* reside in the Lake Chapala area? Estimates range from 10,000 to 30,000 - and everywhere in between.4 Are we able to reduce our cost of housing? Well, that depends on your ability and requirements. Buying a home or condo in this area currently ranges in price from $200,000 to over a million U.S. dollars. Prices are on the increase. Furthermore, real estate housing sales are all cash - there are no mortgages available for foreigners. Rentals are in short supply during the high season (November - April). During my recent visits, the prices for purchasing a home and rental rates increased between August 2018 and October 2018. There also seemed to be a notable increase in the costs for services, food and dining out. Even local realtors we consulted with admit that "housing prices at Lakeside are on the rise." Why?

Supply and demand: With an estimated 10,000 baby boomers in the U.S. reaching retirement age every day until 2030 - and - those in this cohort who have not saved/invested/planned sufficiently for the same; they must now consider reductions in their overall cost of living. 5 Mexico *appears* to provide that opportunity. According to Fannie Mae, Baby Boomers in the U.S. account for forty percent of total U.S. home ownership with $13.5 trillion in home equity.

Yet, the internet is inhabited by virtually every figure you might imagine as it relates to the possibilities for reductions in your overall cost of living by moving to Mexico. The facts are that reality diverges significantly from the *arbitrary quantitative values* that predominate the web narrative, as this is something that is difficult to measure. Don't fall prey to *this artificial and misleading* pitfall. Individual financial circumstances and requirements vary widely. Take the time to plan your financial budgetary requirements, before you explore moving to Mexico (or any other locale). Know *your* numbers. Be real. Budget for the unexpected (travel, healthcare surprises, etc.). *Know before you go.*

The Third Step is to Presume That Which Can't Be Measured Easily Really Isn't Important. This is Blindness

With so many American, Canadian and European retirees considering relocation to Mexico, the assumptions about the purported value of the equity in your home as relocation capital, is a source of unanticipated blindness for too many. Get this measured by a local real estate professional. Get several "market valuations" from different realtors in your local area. Consider a reasonable "time on the market" required to sell your home. Don't forget to account for the realtor commissions and closing costs.

If you think you are simply going to move all your worldly possessions to Mexico...think again. It's costly - very costly. So is storage in the U.S. Consider these costs. Get real numbers. In the Lake Chapala area, contact a local moving and storage company. They have web-based tools to assist you in evaluating the costs, requirements and timeframes (including essential customs compliance on both sides of the border).

Bringing your car to Mexico for your retirement? "Of course we are!" Think again, this is costly, requires proper permits, insurance, and you must either pay a substantial sum for Mexican licensing or get the car out of the country within 6 months of your initial border crossing with the vehicle. Do you have a loan on that vehicle? Are you underwater? If you are a couple, in whose name is the vehicle registered to? Only the registered owner of a vehicle can legally operate it in Mexico. Remember this in your financial and practical *Mexiconsiderations*.

Do you and yours *qualify* for a temporary and/or permanent resident visa in Mexico? What are the certifiable financial and documentary requirements the Mexican Consul in your area deems essential? What are the costs? Timeframes? What are the implications if you do not qualify for anything other than a tourist visa? Have pets? What kind? Can you take them with you? What sort of documentation is required to transport them to your new residence in Mexico? Do your pets require certain vaccinations before travel? Are there veterinarians available? What do they cost?

Are you and yours "digital citizens" who enjoy hassle free internet connectivity, fast downloads and streaming video? Currently, in the Lake Chapala area, I was unable to send my wife in the U.S. a photo via cell phone or my laptop due to the archaic digital infrastructure that currently exists. (There is a plan in place to change that). How much will it cost you to get a satellite TV hook-up? Will you be able to receive all the programming you require? What are acquisition, installation and monthly costs?

Don't fall prey to the blindness that the excitement about the prospect of retiring in Mexico may thrust upon you. Resist the presumption on matters like those addressed above whereby *what can't be measured easily really isn't important.*

The Fourth Step is to Say That Which Can't Be Easily Measured Really Doesn't Exist. This is Suicide

If you are a U.S. citizen contemplating retirement in Mexico, do you believe you are going to be able to somehow reduce your overall healthcare costs by getting rid of costly Medicare supplement plans? Really? What will fill those gaps? If you are required to consume prescription medications to maintain your health, are they available in Mexico? How will you get those meds refilled in Mexico?

Do you have a will? Is it valid in Mexico? What if you purchase real property in Mexico? Is that will still valid in Mexico? If you have a trust, is that trust recognized by the Mexican legal system?

What if you or your spouse experiences a disabling healthcare crisis and/or one that requires major, immediate and ongoing medical interventions? What's your plan for these possibilities? "That'll never happen to us."

Really? What about the unavoidable eventuality of death? What's your plan?

Author Steven Pinker has written: "The difference between a dead body and a living one is that a dead body no longer contains the vital force we call a mind."[1]

Mexconsiderations - contemplating retirement in Mexico - requires mindful measurements - many of which have varying degrees of visibility and escape the consideration they deserve. May this brief article provide you with some helpful tools to guide you along your journey considering Mexico for your retirement years.

NOTES Chapter TWO:

https://www.cbsnews.com/news/more-americans-are-retiring-outside-the-u-s/ - December 27, 2016 -

2 https://money.usnews.com/money/blogs/on-retirement/articles/2017-10-24/8-reasons-mexico-is-americas-favorite-place-to-retire-abroad - October 24, 2017 by Kathleen Peddicord

3 Handy, Charles *The Age of Paradox* Harvard Business School Press © 1994 p. 221

4 https://mexiconewsdaily.com/news/jalisco-earthquakes-felt-in-three-states/

5 http://geo-mexico.com/?p=10612 - "Retirees and "Residential Tourism" - A Case Study of Chapala-Ajijic in Jalisco - January 6, 2014.

6 http://geo-mexico.com/?p=10612 - "Retirees and "Residential Tourism" - A Case Study of Chapala-Ajijic in Jalisco - January 6, 2014.

7 https://seniorplanet.org/aging-out-of-place-in-lake-chapala-mexico/ - April 12, 2017 by Erica Manfred.

8 https://www.housingwire.com/blogs/1-rewired/post/46700-lack-of-retirement-savings-haunts-baby-boomers -

9 Pinker, Steven Blank Slate – The Modern Denial of Human Nature, Penguin Books – An Imprint of Penguin Random House LLC New York, NY Copyright (c) 2002 & 2016 by Steven Pinker, p. 224.

CHAPTER THREE

The Mexodus

North American Retirees Flocking to Mexico

The Mexodus

The New NORMM
NOrth American Retirees Moving to Mexico

(C) 2018 Bill Dahl

Needless to say, the social and political rancor in North America has reached new heights (or lows). In the U.S. political sphere, the November 2018 mid-term elections resulted in the Democratic Party wresting control of the U.S. House of Representatives. The U.S. President's approval ratings hover around 38%. The issue of U.S. immigration reform remains paralyzed amidst political acrimony. Yet, the U.S. President remains adamant about his desire to obtain billions of dollars to build a border wall to keep prospective immigrants out of the U.S. Yet, there's a new norm that has developed.

Obscured by all of the above, is the steady flow North Americans headed south - to Mexico. Frankly, it's an exodus; a MEXODUS. According to CBS News, the number of Americans retiring outside the United States is growing exponentially. Between 2010 and 2015 the number grew 17 percent. The figure is expected to rise during the next 10 years as boomer retirement continues.[1]

According to several sources, Mexico is now considered the preferred retirement home for an estimated 1-2 million American retirees - more than any other country.[1] From the present through 2030, an estimated 10,000 Baby Boomers will achieve retirement age *each day*.[2]

"Where should I retire?" It's a common question in North America as Baby Boomers contemplate how and where they might spend the remainder of this life. For tens of thousands, this question includes destinations outside the U.S. or Canada. Oftentimes, this process involves mulling over Mexico. Every January, the publication International Living, provides retirees with suggestions using their Annual Global Retirement Index. In 2018, Mexico was ranked as the 2nd Best Place to retire by *IL1*. Estimates vary, but it's safe to conclude that a few million Americans and Canadians now reside primarily in Mexico. That's a lot of North Americans who have made the leap.

After completing 2 two week visits to the Guadalajara and Lake Chapala areas in central Mexico in late 2018, I had plenty to consider. The purpose of these trips was to examine the possibility for retirement in this locale; already home to thousands of expat retirees/resident tourists from the U.S., Canada, Europe and the U.K. What motivated my wife and me to invest in considering Mexico? We had several. We're not alone. During these recent exploratory visits, we had the opportunity to speak with dozens upon dozens of North American baby boomers in Mexico. Some were already residing there. Others were exploring the possibilities as we were. Our question was: "What inspires retiring North American baby boomers to consider Mexico as their retirement home?" Here's what they told us:

1. *Reduce My Cost of Living* - As study after study indicates, North American Baby Boomers are ill prepared financially for retirement. This "lack of financial preparedness" has become the primary cause of anxiety among Boomers.2

  According to *International Living*, you can live on U.S. $1,865 per month in Mexico including rent, utilities, groceries, entertainment, healthcare, household help and incidentals. For a couple, the figure moves to an estimated $2,500 per month.1 Again, costs are relative. Want to live in a tourist area near a Mexican beach on the sea? Your costs will be significantly higher. The same is true for areas in Mexico where North American retirees are already well established like the Lake Chapala/Ajijic area and San Miguel Allende. The current peso to the dollar foreign exchange reality makes reducing the cost of living even more practical (currently 20.5 pesos to one U.S. dollar in early December 2018).

2. *A Better Climate* - For many, the motivation to move toward a better climate and retire the snow shovel, winter clothing, umbrella, and avoid sleet, ice, humidity, excessive heat, and the like was a common reply. Of course, Mexico is a massive geographic area. However, the varieties of improved climate choices within the country make it attractive to retiring baby boomers.

3. *More Affordable Healthcare* - Mexico, particularly when compared to the U.S. has a vastly more affordable healthcare environment.2 Of course,

this depends upon one's current medical requirements and those that may arise in the future. No, Medicare is not valid for medical treatment outside the U.S. Thus, you must rely on cash and qualifying for available Mexican healthcare coverage for those who hold both temporary and permanent visas. Of course, for treatment requiring Medicare coverage, you can return to the U.S. for the same.

4. *A Cultural Adventure* - A common response was the desire for a cultural adventure. Mexico's proximity to Canada and the U.S. provides just that. From food, to landscapes to architecture, language, the arts and the people - Mexico possesses what North American retirees seeking new cultural experiences are after.

Baby Boomers have been characterized as those who "make smart decisions based on available resources." They are independent and "make up their own minds and determine what is most valuable or significant."3 Moving to Mexico for retirement appears to have become the new norm for North American boomers. There is no wall that can prevent the flow of North American retirees relocating to Mexico - along with their substantial economic contributions to the Mexican economy. Perhaps you and those you know might join the MEXODUS?

CHAPTER FOUR

Lake Chapala – The Fifth Risk

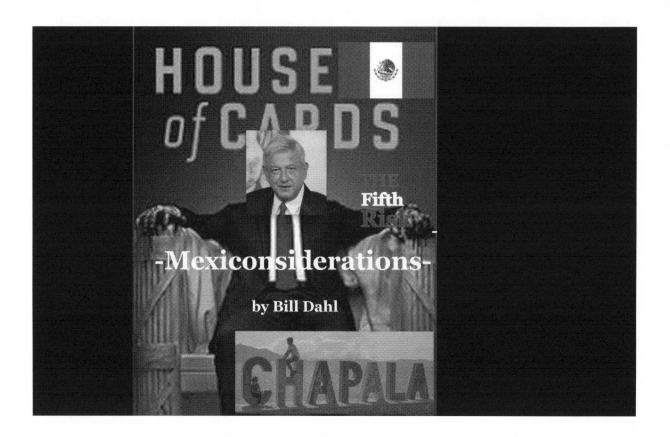

During my visit to the Guadalajara and Lake Chapala areas in October/November 2018 I brought along a new book; The Fifth Risk by one of my favorite writers, New York Times bestselling author Michael Lewis. On the final page of the book is a quote that captures its' essence: "*It's what you fail to imagine that kills you.*"1

How is this pertinent to *Mexiconsiderations*? Stay with me.

On October 29, 2018 the Lake Chapala Reporter published a piece about the results of a Lake Chapala water quality study presented during a seminar at the Jesuit University of Guadalajara. According to one official, the study indicated characterized the detected levels of arsenic and coliforms as *worrisome* (exceeding safety levels identified by the World Health Organization). This same article stated: "Wastewater treatment plants are <u>NOT</u> working (Lakeside municipalities cannot afford electricity payments to operate them). Thus, wastewater continues to be discharged into the Lake."2

Holy crap, I said to myself. I recalled how unusual it is to see people swimming in the lake. I wondered *why*. I decided to look into this public health issue further.

On November 8, 2018 The Lake Chapala Reporter disclosed that Chapala had not paid for water sanitation in three years. The CEA - the State Water Commission - demanded payment of 6 million pesos for their management of Chapala's wastewater treatment facilities. Chapala had only 900,000 pesos budgeted.3 Chapala has recently asked the Government of Jalisco for a loan to repay these 3 years of past due bills for wastewater treatment. A week before this disclosure, it was reported that the rainy season had added so much water to the lake that in Riberas del Pilar, groundwater was being contaminated due to overflowing septic tanks.4

As I investigated this issue further, a quote from author Michael Lewis kept ringing in my head: "*the fifth risk is the risk a society runs when it falls into the habit of responding to long-term risks with short-term solutions.*"5 It turns out that the public health and environmental concerns contained in the Lake Chapala region have been studied extensively over the years. Yet, little, if any, comprehensive and coordinated efforts have been implemented to address this multi-dimensional miasma. Certainly, no plan is currently in place that will provide scientifically verifiable results regarding the comprehensive environmental restoration of the Lake Chapala basin. On the contrary, the situation has become vastly more serious. It would be unfair to blame Mexico and the communities that surround Lake Chapala for this failure. The consequences of The Fifth Risk are apparent throughout each and every society in human civilization. Yet, that's no excuse to continue kicking the can down the road versus garnering the essential attention and action of the federal government in Mexico to begin to enact the required multi-faceted solution(s).

I contacted Gabriel Vazquez Sanchez, General Director of the Intermunicipal Association for the Protection of the Environment and Sustainable Development of Lake Chapala (AIPROMADES). He characterized the current public health and environmental situation in Lake Chapala as follows: "*an emergency that should be addressed at all levels of government.*"6 Again, I heard myself mutter, *Holy crap*!

A study published in August 2018 concluded: "Lake Chapala is the main source of drinking water for over 4-million inhabitants. We concluded that it will be difficult to continue to use the lake as the main source of freshwater for the Guadalajara metropolitan area without substantial interventions."7 Another study revealed the level of fecal coliforms measured in Lake Chapala "indicates the existence of untreated wastewater discharges from municipalities or the low efficiencies of wastewater treatment plants."8 The most riveting study concerned the health of children - the majority was between the ages of five and nine in this specific study.9 CDK (Chronic Kidney Disease) was found to be endemic in a specific population of children residing in a community adjacent to Lake Chapala. The term endemic refers to a disease or condition routinely found in a particular area and among certain group of people This particular study began in 2016. The results were published in 2017. The findings are alarming: 68% of the children studied were diagnosed with stage 3a or 3b of Chronic Kidney Disease (3a = mild to moderate/3b= moderate to severe). The rate of CKD in this particular studied population is 3-5 times higher than others. The researchers also found traces of heavy metals (mercury and lead) present in the urine samples of the children.10

In this article, you have heard people declare the public health and environmental reality in Lake Chapala to be one requiring immediate, *substantial interventions* and *an emergency that should be addressed at all levels of government*. Perhaps you think this set of public health concerns is for indigenous populations only. Well, you'd be wrong. In the study involving the children above, all 451 kids tested positive for the insecticide dimethoate - and the popular weed killer glyphosate; a positive test for the presence of pesticides. The researchers determined that the same levels of pesticides were resident in 50 year old men and two year old infants. Transmission was via air currents. "There are pesticides in the lake. When the water heats, it evaporates, and the air currents pass from the lake to the population."11 This includes the thousands of expats who reside in the Lake Chapala area. There is no immunity to public health hazards on our planet - no matter your nationality, income, gender, political party affiliations, religion or sexual identity.

Michael Lewis wrote, "*The risk we should most fear is not the risk we easily imagine. It is the risk that we don't.*"12 That may be true. However, when the public health and environmental risks are apparent and require human action to resolve - and *we* fail to respond accordingly, that is not a failure of the imagination. It is a failure of the human will.

What's THE ROOT OF THE PROBLEM, According to Enrique Lira, a coordinator of the Socio-Environmental Forum in Guadalajara: "What is genetic is the disinterest of the authorities. They deny the problem as their predecessors did. It's like avoiding responsibility is in their genes."13 Well, although the U.S. remains saddled with a President who continues to deny the reality of the ongoing public health and environmental degradation posed by both climate change and the intentional destruction of a robust environmental regulatory enforcement apparatus (it may be another expression of the cognitive and genetic defects of this guy) - Mexico is not. On the contrary, the recent election of Andrés Manuel López Obrador (AMLO in September

2018) was accompanied by a strategic plan to clean up Mexico's environment.14 This should unequivocally include the restoration and re-imagination of a seminally important body of water in Mexico... Lake Chapala and its' tributaries; upgrading wastewater treatment facilities, and establishing the monitoring, infrastructure, and quality improvements for the distribution of clean drinking water for the current population - and for generations to come.

THE FUTURE OF LAKE CHAPALA will not be due to a failure of the imagination. It will be determined by a coordinated chorus of voices demanding that the fifth risk must be avoided - where *the fifth risk is the risk a society runs when it falls into the habit of responding to long-term risks with short-term solutions."15* There are no short-term solutions available for the comprehensive remediation of the public health and environmental risks posed by the current conditions in the Lake Chapala region. On the contrary, succumbing to the fifth risk has caused the current reality. Perhaps, the expats residing in the Chapala region, along with the Mexican people, can come together to be an integral part of a uniquely effective chorus. It will be a process, not an event. Yet, it can be one that will become an enduring source of national pride and international collaboration - for the benefit of ALL stakeholders. Nothing is more powerful than coordinated and collaborative international advocacy led by those determined to eradicate the legitimate threats to their piece of paradise on this planet.

It may be another episode of falling prey to the fifth risk if this does not occur...a *Mexiconsideration.*

For me, I am hoping the local Mexicans and ex-pats residing in the Lake Chapala region rise up together, and insure that the required remediation becomes a reality. It will take decades...

CHAPTER FIVE

NaturAMLO

The <u>A</u>mazing <u>M</u>exico <u>L</u>eadership <u>O</u>pportunity

Drip, Drip, Drip...

Pulitzer Prize winning author and scientist Jared Diamond[1] has written; "societies fail to perceive a problem is when it takes the form of a slow trend concealed by wide up-and-down fluctuations."[2] Perhaps that's why our planet's annual seasonal fluctuations obscure the reality of climate change. Furthermore, human perception is wired to recognize the apparent. When it comes to water quality, associated public health maladies, on ongoing ecosystem degradation - these are "slow trends concealed" from our everyday observations because they are less than apparent to us. As Diamond writes in another of his works; "By the time that the signs of decline are clear enough to convince everybody, it may be too late to save the species or habitat."[3] With water, the decline in its quality and supply, the emergence of related public health maladies, economic decline, the degradation of surrounding ecosystems, and the loss of species, some endemic, contained therein. The destruction of essential water resources that support healthy human habitation, and the associated, strategically important economies is a slow trend; a drip, drip, drip process.

Water resources worldwide are under tremendous stress. The availability of freshwater is anticipated to become the primary risk associated with economic growth, political stability, and human survival in the near term. Mexico is no exception to this reality.

The Lerma-Lake Chapala-Santiago basin in Mexico provides millions of people and associated economic interests with the primary water resource they require. Its viability is currently under siege after decades upon decades of mismanagement and neglect. Guadalajara, Mexico's second largest city and the 4 million + residents of the broader region are fundamentally sustained by this distinctly imperiled water resource. Guadalajara is considered the bright shining star of Mexico's economic engine of the future. (Guadalajara has a geographic footprint and population equivalent to that of Madrid, the capital of Spain).How's that going to turn out with no water in that engine?

According to the World Bank: "Water resources management is one of Mexico's most urgent environmental and resource problems, and one that imposes heavy costs on the economy." 4 This WB study also observes that the decreases in available water in Mexico have increased pollution accompanied by increased demand. The report goes on to point out: "Nevertheless, significant challenges remain, particularly in terms of improving water services and quality and defining the regulations required to implement the established legal and institutional framework. Over half of Mexican households still lack reliable and continuous water services. For most of the country, municipal effluents remain untreated and irrigation systems have rates of inefficiency that exceed 50 percent."5

Well, that particular World Bank study was 12 years ago. Yet, its conclusions remain valid, and require updating to verify the current extent and nature of the damage. In 2015, Mexico established The National Water Commission (Comisión Nacional del Agua aka CONAGUA). Its purpose is to be the administrative and technical advisory commission of Mexico's Ministry of the Environment and Natural Resources (SEMARNAT). More specifically, CONAGUA administers Mexico's waters, the nation's hydrological apparatus, and performs associated social development activities. So what have been the substantive, meaningful, tangible, positive, sustainable results of studies, reports, meetings, conferences and commissions? Frankly, for the residents of Mexico...honestly?...nada. Actually, the water quality, environmental degradation and public health hazards have actually worsened.

The Lerma-Lake Chapala-Santiago basin is the most glaring example of the absence of meaningful and urgent Federal government intervention. Flows into the lake transport toxic sediments from the upper basin into the depths of the lake. Untreated sewage, run-off and wastewater are routinely discharged into the lake, scientifically verified presence of heavy metals in humans, fish, foods and flora are apparent, municipalities cannot afford the electricity required to operate sewage and wastewater treatment plants, the lake is infested by water hyacinths, and the incidence of Chronic Kidney disease remains the 2nd worst in the world, and in some locations around the lake, the incidence of CKD is 3-5 times greater than any other places on the planet. Need I say more?

What's the problem? Like many countries, Mexico is struggling with population increases, industries requiring water, lack of adequately constructed and maintained sites for disposal of toxins, poor water quality assessment and delivery infrastructure, regulatory inefficiencies, and limitations on financial resources.6 Translation: The problem is multi-faceted. The required solution is multi-dimensional as well.

Hope or Hype?

Yet, there's hope. On December 1, 2018 Andrés Manuel López Obrador aka AMLO was elected as the new President of Mexico. Accompanying his election was his pledge to clean up the environment (among other issues) and a renewed focus on restoring the water resources of his nation via a splashy, bold document entitled "NaturAMLO."

After a major national election in almost any country, people are filled with hope, buoyed by all the hype filled promises that inflated the narrative of the election.

In his book, *Collapse - How Societies Choose To Fail Or Succeed*, Jared Diamond suggests that societies fail due to the cumulative effects of 4 basic choices; "failure to anticipate a problem (anticipation), failure to perceive it once it has arisen (perception), failure to attempt to solve it after it has been perceived (failure to act), and failure to succeed in attempts to solve it (failure to succeed)."7 Regarding water supply, water quality, the emergence associated diseases, and the degradation of ecosystems Mexico, like many other countries, has succumbed to the failures in each of the stages identified by Diamond.

Yet, President AMLO has an immediate advantage over his predecessors. Guided by his NaturAMLO agenda, his choices will determine the future of the strategically essential waters of the Lake Chapala basin for the Mexican people, and his nation's economic prowess. As the title of Diamond's book indicates, Societies *choose* to fail or succeed. Will NaturAMLO be hype or will it embody the demonstrable leadership so boldly proclaimed by the new Mexican President by the immediate decisions and choices he makes – translating the hopes of the Mexican people into reality.

What might these decisions and choices look like?

A Pathway to Progress:

It took decades for the degradation of the Lerma-Chapala-Santiago basin to come about. It will also be a process to stop the deterioration and begin to restore this strategically essential resource for the Mexican people and the country of Mexico. What might this look like? Perhaps some of the following suggestions will be helpful in providing a phased framework within which this process can succeed.

I. Immediate -

A. The issuance of an emergency Executive Order by Mexican President AMLO designating the Lerma-Chapala-Santiago basin as a national NaturAMLO site.

B. The term NaturAMLO refers to both an **A**mazing **M**exico **L**eadership **O**pportunity for Andrés Manuel López Obrador and embodies the concrete actions that declare the **A**melioration **M**andate for **L**ake Chapala's **O**versight

C. By Presidential executive order, provide a budget and initial, emergency funding to complete the items identified herein as Immediate and Short Term objectives.

D. The immediate establishment of the an official, Federal, Mexican Government Agency - The NaturAMLO Agency - to evaluate, supervise, fund, coordinate, administrate and rehabilitate designated AMLO sites, as declared by the Mexican President. These sites shall be areas that contain known and scientifically reasonably suspected hazards to human health and require strategically important rehabilitation of environmental degradation for the benefit and future of the country of Mexico.

E. Empower the Mexican President to authorize additional funding to designated NaturAMLO sites.

F. Immediately prohibit access to known sites of human health hazards - one example is Agual Caliente spring waters - and others as identified by the NaturAMLO staff in cooperation with designated experts in multi-disciplinary fields retained for ongoing scientific guidance.

G. Establish a board of public health and environmental experts empowered to advise the NaturAMLO staff as to priorities, methodological considerations for additional, essential studies, the acquisition and deployment of essential scientific environmental measurement and data acquisition devices, and serve to oversee the completion of scientific studies approved by NaturAMLO and the public dissemination of their results - and recommend further scientific remediation modalities when and wherever required.

H. Prohibit the spraying of pesticides on water hyacinths that inhabit the lake by any party.

I. Nationalize the operation of the municipal and Jalisco state operated sewage and wastewater treatment plants around Lake Chapala. The current municipal/state of Jalisco government entities do not that the funds and staff to operate and maintain these facilities effectively. Currently, the lakeside municipalities do not possess the financial resources required to pay for the electrical power required to operate and maintain them. Currently, it is essential to explore the use alternative sources of energy for their operation to reduce their operating costs.

J. Provide an immediate and ongoing supply of clean drinking water to the most at-risk communities - including Agua Caliente, Mezcala, San Pedro Itzicán, El Salto and Juanacatlán - as identified by Enrique Lira coordinator of the Socio-Environmental Forum in Guadalajara. Furthermore, Lakeside communities require a comprehensive intervention in their water resources, including sources, conduction, storage, purification and delivery infrastructure.

K. Establish a Chronic Kidney Disease diagnostic, monitoring and treatment center in Mezcala to provide medical services to affected populations - including the provision of current, state of the art medical devices required to treat a range of patients who suffer from various stages of kidney disease. According to Gabriel Vazquez

Sanchez, Director of AIPROMADES8 in Guadalajara: "The most critical sites are in the territory of the municipality of Poncitlán. Placing this center in Mezcala would be strategically significant and would have a profound, positive social impact."

L. Enact federal regulatory legislation specific to this AMLO site. This includes fines and legal consequences for those who breach the federally mandated and administered AMLO site protocols. Deploy AMLO site government overseers who have the official legal authority to monitor compliance with, and enforcement of, this legislation locally, on-site.

M. Deploy an additional 21 water hyacinth *(Eichhornia crassipes aka liros)* harvesting machines to Lake Chapala, fully staffed by trained operators. (There are only 2 harvesting machines at present) Furthermore, make certain that adequate and essential equipment is available to transport the harvested water hyacinths to a designated disposal site so that mounds of harvested water hyacinths do not accumulate on the lakeshore, delayed by the essential disposal transportation to the designated disposal sites. There are also shredding machines owned and operated by the State Rural Development Secretary. However, shredding the water hyacinths is not a solution. The total extraction of the plant is required. Furthermore, it is also necessary to complete an analysis of the chemicals and heavy metals contained in the extracted plants, to ensure their safety level to remanufacture them into compost or require their disposal at safe disposal sites.

N. The infestation of water hyacinths is not the only invasive species issue. Studies have identified 7 species of aquatic invasive plants. These invaders make root or that float, and their geometric growth alters the Lake conditions. Interestingly, the water hyacinth or lily, is no longer the most abundant species. Pistia stratiotes, water lettuce, which appears to be more resistant to the increasing temperature. The seven invasive aquatic species in Lake Chapala identified by scientists include: Hydrocotyle ranunculoides, Berula erecta, Juncus effusus, Lemma gibba, Typha latifolia, Eichhornia Crassipes and Pistia stratiotes. These infestations in Lake Chapala must be arrested due to their multi-dimensional negative impacts on the ecosystem. These deleterious effects include: blocking inflows and outflows, hampering recreation and fishing, reducing natural currents and water movement, reducing the amount of dissolved oxygen, and retarding the penetration of sunlight. These realities of water hyacinth infestation complicate the essential production of phytoplankton and the health and reproduction of resident fish species. They also provide superb breeding grounds for noxious organisms like mosquitoes that are known carriers of both the Dengue and Zika viruses. It has also been suggested that the hyacinths absorb heavy metals absorbed from Lake Chapala - attributed to industrial waste deposited in the Lerma River that flows into Lake Chapala.9

O. Establish and distribute public information materials to fully inform the local populations of the Lerma-Chapala-Santiago basin about its designation as a NaturAMLO site, and provide incentives to them to cooperate and comply with this national initiative. Create and distribute this information to schools throughout the designated area, and adjacent communities.

P. Recovery of the meaningful RAMSAR Site designation for Lake Chapala is imperative. A management plan that allows for the conservation, nesting and refuge sites of the migratory birds is of international importance. Lake Chapala is a wildlife refuge for migratory waterfowl. The Lake provides the habitat for feeding, hibernation and breeding. The Lake is also home to numerous species of fish, including *Menidia contrerasi, Menidia sphyraena, Ictalurus dugesii,* and *Menidia promelas.* The habitat provides support for endangered species of birds including *Botaurus lentiginosus* and *Rallus limicola,* and mammals like the Mexican Long-nosed Bat (*Leptonycteris nivalis*) and the Collared peccary (*Tayassu tajacu*), as well as Puma (*Felis concolor*) - which is also endangered.10

II. Short Term: Completion **Within 9 Months of Declar**ing the Lerma-Chapala-Santiago basin as a Federally Designated AMLO Site

A. Complete a review of the public health and environmental studies completed by the scientific communities over the past 20 years. Identify:

a. Scientific evidence that confirms both public health and environmental hazards that require immediate rehabilitation and eradication actions. Define the appropriate scientific remediation modalities, including the essential monitoring of ongoing scientific data collection moving toward the achievement of the public and environmental improvement benchmarks.

b. Identify the *absence* of essential scientific studies that must be completed to ascertain the multi-causal factors whose cumulative effects contribute to the current malady. Issue RFP's, and evaluate the submitted RFP's for these essential studies that have yet to be completed. Fund and initiate these scientific studies on or before one year from the date of designation of the Lerma-Chapala-Santiago basin as a NaturAMLO site.

B. Deploy the essential arrays of scientific measurement devices throughout Lake Chapala basin that are currently lacking. These include: resident water quality measurement devices, measurements devices where any treated effluent is discharged into the lake, examine and deploy water quality measurement arrays at current, known sites where storm water run-off is discharged routinely into the Lake, deploy air quality testing arrays around the Lake to ascertain the degree of evaporation of toxins (e.g., pesticide residues) from lake waters that are the disbursed onto adjacent landscape and human populations, obtain core sediment samples at numerous locations within the lake body to determine the current identity of, location and concentrations of heavy metals). This process must include the analysis of sludge and sediments via topobathymetry that measure the cure, actual state of the soils. This has not been done for more than twenty years

C. Initiate a comprehensive scientific examination of the use of pesticides and fertilizers throughout the Lerma-Chapala-Santiago basin as a NaturAMLO region. (See Corazon de la Tierra, 201311)

D. Initiate a comprehensive scientific examination of the presence of toxins hazardous to human health in the fish species throughout the the Lerma-Chapala-Santiago basin.

E. Initiate a comprehensive scientific examination of the presence of toxins hazardous to human health in the agricultural products grown, harvested, sold and consumed throughout the Lerma-Chapala-Santiago basin.

F. Feedback Loop - Ongoing Public and scientific disclosures as scientific results from assessment and remediation efforts are available for public consumption. At a minimum, progress reports for this NaturAMLO site should be issued every 6 months.

III. Long Term: Completion Within 48 Months of Declaring the Le**rma-Chapala-Santiago basin as a** Federally Designated AMLO Site

The Lerma-Lake Chapala-Santiago basin is a unique national treasure of phenomenal beauty and strategic importance to Mexico as a nation. Yet, we know the region remains vulnerable to misuse, exploitation and ongoing threats to its survival. Degradation of the region and this ecosystem happened over the course of more than a century. Even with the resiliency of nature, discernible widespread improvements will also take time. The goals, objectives, measures of progress and other efforts identified in the NaturAMLO Plan will help ensure quantifiable annual outputs are in place that will lead to long-term restoration outcomes, even if such outcomes will not be immediately measurable on an ecosystem scale. Degradation is a process. So is the rehabilitation of the same.

A. Long term requirements for the restoration of any ecosystem evolve over time, as the results of essential scientific measurements dictate.

B. Consult with the international community to garner the experience of other comparable ecosystems that have been restored. Implement a "best practices" mechanism to inject successful approaches, interventions, and technologies elsewhere into the Lerma-Lake Chapala-Santiago basin NaturAMLO initiative.

C. Dredging – Removal of heavy metals from Lake/River bottom sediments may be essential. Replacement soil may be required.

D. Longitudinal Studies are essential.

E. Annual Public Disclosures of the Previous 12 months Efforts, Results and Plans for the Upcoming year are required.

F. Review readily available comparable interventions. See: https://www.glri.us/sites/default/files/glri-action-plan-fy2010-fy2014-20100221-41pp.pdf and https://www.epa.gov/greatlakes/restoring-great-lakes as examples.

G. Based upon the urgency and strategic importance this situation demands, the initiation of the search for qualified, experienced, strategic partners - on an international scale - who can provide on-site scientific assistance, the provision of required measurement devices, and sources of ongoing funding - are essential.

In conclusion, national treasures require the leadership, choices and treasury of a nation to maintain and restore them as enduring, legitimate displays of of national pride and vision. May President Andrés Manuel López Obrador's NaturAMLO priority be treated as *the* **A**mazing **M**exico **L**eadership **O**pportunity and be translated from hype into hope by virtue of the President's declaration of the Lerma-Lake Chapala-Santiago basin with the honor of being nationally designated as the **A**melioration **M**andate for **L**ake Chapala's **O**versight.

Mexico's Lake Chapala is the largest lake in the country, the 3rd largest in Latin America, and said to be the 2nd highest in the Americas, surpassed only by Lake Titicaca. It is the primary source of the water supply for the greater Guadalajara metropolitan area. Its strategic importance to the nation of Mexico us unparalleled. It is the largest water source in Mexico. Millions of people, plant and animal species, and the viability of the nation's economy depend upon the enactment of an aggressive, comprehensive, and coordinated strategy designed for its restoration.

Such is the current opportunity for Mexico. Without water resource rehabilitation, humanity will be sunk. Mexico is no exception. Renowned author and psychologist Steven Pinker[12] has written: "The nature of reality does not dictate the way that reality is represented in people's minds. [13]" Thus, interpretation depends upon "what we choose to focus on and what we choose to ignore."[14]

Will the new President of Mexico Andrés Manuel López Obrador focus on the implementation of a comprehensive strategy dedicated to the remediation of the public health and environmental hazards that currently inhabit the Lerma-Lake Chapala-Santiago basin? Or will he choose, as his predecessors have, to continue to ignore this urgent reality?

The *choice* is President Obrador's.

Perhaps Mexico will lead the way...it's a **A**mazing **M**exico **L**eadership **O**pportunity for Mexico!

The whole world is watching.

Chapter SIX

CUTE or CURE?

Lake Chapala Is A Sick Puppy

The term "Clean Up The Environment" (hereinafter "cute") has become a phrase used by politicians to denote a concern that may play well at the polls, but rarely turns into measurable improvements for the ecosystem. On December 1, 2018 Mexico installed their new President, Andrés Manuel López Obrador (AMLO). His election garnered widespread electoral support by virtue of his comprehensive environmental restoration agenda for Mexico entitled NaturAMLO. The whole world is watching.

For AMLO's administration(as well as many others around this planet), the question becomes one of delivering tangible environmental and public health improvements for his nation, or becoming just another politician playing the cute card. Yet, AMLO and Mexico have a distinct advantage; a cure for cute.

The Lerma-Lake Chapala-Santiago basin in Mexico is a sick puppy. Lake Chapala is located some 35 minutes south of Guadalajara, Mexico's second largest city, with over 4 million residents. The lake is situated in the state of Jalisco in western Mexico. Jalisco has an estimated 6.3 million inhabitants, 60% of whom reside in the state capital of Guadalajara, with the remainder dispersed among urban and rural areas in the region. Unemployment among adults who are actively seeking work is low (approximately 2%), while annual per capita income is approximately US $6000. The primary employers in the state of Jalisco are agriculture (11%), manufacturing/industrial (25%) and the services sector (31%) and sectors. Guadalajara is considered to be an economic engine for Mexico - and one with even more positive economic potential in the future. According to one source, "Guadalajara had the second strongest economic potential of any major North American city, with only Chicago scoring higher for sheer economic potential."1

Lake Chapala is the source of drinking water for 60% of Guadalajara's requirements, and a few million others. This Lake is the largest body of freshwater in Mexico spanning some 48 miles in length and 12 miles across. The region touts its ranking as the second best climate in the world. Surrounded by lush green vegetation, the Sierra Madre mountains, fertile soils, and magnificent vistas - it is a veritable Garden of Eden. Fishermen feed their families from their catches in the lake and sell them in local markets. Fruits and vegetables are grown in abundance in the area. It is a weekend getaway destination for residents of metropolitan Guadalajara. The Lake Chapala region is also inhabited by tens of thousands of Canadians, Americans, and Europeans who have chosen "Lakeside" as their retirement home. Thus, the Lakeside area (the north shore sector of the Lake) is truly international in composition. Yet, there are scientifically determined public health and environmental problems in paradise.

Recent studies have identified wastewater treatment plants discharging untreated effluent into the lake, resulting in measurements of unhealthy levels of fecal coliform. The cities and/or agencies required to operate these facilities don't have the money to pay for the electricity required to operate them. Other studies have identified the presence of heavy metals in lake water and the sediment in the lake. Pesticides containing the likes of glyphosate (Think "Round-Up") have been found in humans living around the lake. The pesticide source has been attributed to the evaporation of lake water and the subsequent dispersal onto local inhabitants via air currents (wind) and precipitation (rain). Septic systems in some areas are overflowing and contaminating ground water. Children in a specific village adjacent to the lake have been diagnosed with varying degrees of Chronic Kidney Disease at rates deemed 3-5 times greater than comparable populations. There is nothing cute about children medically diagnosed as living perilously on the downward slope toward ESRD - end stage renal disease - the final stage of kidney disease.

Chronic Kidney Disease (CKD) is an increasing source of concern for public health officials worldwide. However, for Mexico, the matter has become increasingly alarming. A recent study determined that between 1990 and

2013, the CKD incidence in Mexico translated into increases to >130% in standardized years of life lost and disability-adjusted life-years (DALY); the second highest DALY CKD ratio in the world.2 A 2018 study concluded: "It is of paramount importance to consider CKD a public health priority and to implement a comprehensive program of prevention and treatment of this illness."3

Back to Lake Chapala. According to the World Health Organization "Globally, almost 800 million people lack access to safe water and 2.5 billion lack access to optimal sanitation. In low- and middle-income countries, waterborne and pestilent diseases associated with poor hygiene and sanitation are major causes of acute kidney injury and chronic kidney disease."4 Unfortunately, in the Lake Chapala basin, poverty inhabits paradise. Those without clean drinking water due to socio-economic realities, continue to rely on lake water and other drainages/sources that surround the lake. Public health, environmental and humanitarian advocates continue to press government officials to intervene and begin the remediation process. Inspired by the public health hazards resident amidst the contamination of the Lerma-Chapala-Santiago basin, advocates have repeatedly called upon the Jalisco Health Secretariat (SSJ) to complete an epidemiological study in areas known to be sources of public health hazards.5 They receive the typical "cute" responses intended to pacify them from these government authorities, and a myriad of others.

Frankly, Lake Chapala is a national treasure of Mexico. It is a global treasure. It is an area inhabited by people from all around the globe. The health and welfare of millions are dependent upon the restoration of these waters and this basin. The conundrum legitimately demands a cure versus any more cute treatment. **C**hapala **U**rgently **R**equires the **E**xtraordinary: a national political directive that moves from the lip-service of cute, to the demonstrable remediation and enduring pride delivered by the CURE. Translation: **C**omprehend the **U**rgency to **R**ehabilitate the **E**cosystem. The administration of Mexico's President Andrés Manuel López Obrador

(AMLO) has the opportunity to declare that Lake Chapala deserves the designation as a site for the CURE. Perhaps this will be the first tangible step in the roll-out of AMLO's NaturAMLO promise to the people of Mexico. I certainly hope so.

How will President Andrés Manuel López Obrador treat this sick puppy?

The whole world is watching.

CHAPTER SEVEN

KABOOM

Calculating the Economic Costs of Baby Boomers retiring to Mexico

The term *boomerang* is considered a noun and a verb. As a noun, it is defined as a curved flat piece of wood that can be thrown so as to return to the thrower, traditionally used by Australian Aborigines as a hunting weapon. As a verb, *boomerang* means a plan or action that results in a return to the originator, often with negative consequences.1

One of the overlooked, unanticipated consequences of social, economic and political policies is that they inherently possess a boomerang effect; they return to the sender with negative consequences. A current example of this phenomenon are the negative consequences U.S. President Donald Trump's range of policies have thrust upon a major demographic cohort in the U.S.: The Baby Boomers.

U.S. Baby Boomers are retiring – in droves. Some estimates suggest up to 10,000 a day. U.S. boomers have been characterized as "having a - you only live once" mindset. Boomers have been uniquely focused on having personally and professionally productive retirements."2 They seem driven to try new experiences and stay active throughout their golden years." Boomers, along with GenXers, hold what are described as "consistently or mostly liberal views than have conservative positions."3 Another observer notes: "Whether it's for economic viability or to gain companionship, seniors' willingness to think outside the box is driving the growth of unconventional housing solutions."4 One of the experiences boomers are living in their golden years involves moving south – to Mexico. Why? What are the economic roots and implications of this movement?

According to a recent study, U.S. boomers are ill-prepared to maintain their current lifestyle in the U.S. in their retirement years. An estimated one-half of U.S. boomer retirees will be solely dependent upon their Social Security income. Just under 25% of boomers have no retirement savings whatsoever, while 42% will have saved less than $100,000. [5] Once referred to as the wealthiest generation in U.S. history, the estimates of current U.S. boomer wealth ranges from U.S. $4.6 trillion to $30 trillion dollars.[6] Whatever the exact figure may be, boomer holdings of residential properties comprise a significant portion of that wealth.[7] U.S. Boomers ages 65 and over have an estimated "extractable" home equity figure of $3.1 trillion dollars.[8] With the peso currently trading at 20.3 pesos to one U.S. dollar, the financial attraction of Mexico as a retirement destination for U.S. boomers is both legitimate and alluring. Perhaps Donald Trump has fallen prey to what NY Times bestselling author Michael Lewis has referred to as the fifth risk: *It's what you fail to imagine that kills you.*"[9]

Between 2016 and 2017, 2016-to 2017, Mexico was the unequivocal primary travel destination of choice for U.S. residents, rising 12% from 31 million to 35 million during those years alone.[10] Interestingly enough, it has been noted that more U.S. residents are moving to Mexico than Mexicans moving to the U.S.[11] Estimates of Mexican revenues from tourism are estimated at U.S. $13.3 billion[12] in 2016. The recent growth of the tourism industry in Mexico is remarkable. It reached new heights in 2018[13] and is currently the fifth largest source of revenue for Mexico.[14] The fastest growing segment of the Mexican economy is tourism (among others). Tourism contributes an estimated half of Mexican GDP. For Mexico, the primary source of foreign exchange, after remittances and petroleum exports, is tourism.[15]

The strategic importance of the Mexico-U.S. economic interchange is of vital importance, to both nations. The U.S. is Mexico's largest trading partner. For the U.S., Mexico ranks third as a source of U.S. imports and second as an export market for the U.S. In 2017, Mexican exports to the U.S. total approximately 37% of Mexico's GDP or 80% of all of Mexico's exports.[16] What these figures do not reflect is the export of the purchasing power of U.S. Boomers now flowing to Mexico for their retirement years.

Incredibly, the U.S. government does not maintain statistics on the number of U.S. citizens living abroad. The U.S. State Department estimates the current figure to be in the ballpark of 9 million.17 The number of U.S. citizens residing in Mexico ranges from 1.7 million to over 2 million.18 It is safe to say that "Mexico is the country with the largest community of US citizens living outside the United States;"19 more than any other country in the world.20

As I have written elsewhere, the steady stream of North American boomers headed to Mexico for retirement is a Mexodus. It is reasonable to believe these numbers will continue to escalate. The primary motivation of boomers headed to/living in Mexico is to reduce their overall cost of living, among others. The economic contribution of boomers who make the leap south to Mexico for their retirement years will be a windfall for Mexico. Their departure may also contribute to unanticipated factors taking the wind out of the sails of the U.S. economy. What can the U.S. do to address this phenomenon? Frankly, not much, if anything. It's too late to assemble a legitimate "affordable healthcare" system that will entice boomers to stay. A significant Medicare and Social Security increase? Fat chance - politically. Eliminate political rancor and polarization in the U.S....not happening. For boomers driven by "economic viability, a willingness to think outside the box regarding unconventional housing solutions, to try new experiences, and stay active throughout their golden years"21 – well, Mexico is terribly attractive.

What might Mexico do to capitalize on this once in a generation economic opportunity? First, to fail to target this economic windfall would be an avoidable strategic oversight. The new, Mexican federal government, the National Office of Tourism in Mexico, and cities throughout Mexico should become focused on this bonanza and engage in outreach marketing to this North American boomer market. A comprehensive examination of any current, non-essential barriers for relocation to Mexico by boomers is a superb suggestion. Mexico, like many other countries, has public health and environmental hazards that need to be addressed. This agenda should be elevated to a national priority, as identified in Mexico's NaturAMLO initiative, touted by new Mexican President Andrés Manuel López Obrador. Finally, Mexico should consider enacting a set of incentives to attract North American boomers to relocate to Mexico.

For Trump, the boomerang he has thrown at Mexico is bound to return to him with a myriad of unanticipated, ongoing, negative, economic and socio-political consequences. For Mexico, Trump's boomerang is bound to return economic windfalls for years to come.

KABOOM!

CHAPTER EIGHT

Corruption in Mexico

An Interview with Mexico Corruption Scholar

Dr. Jose Ivan Rodriguez-Sanchez

Lake Chapala Basin - Environmental & Public Health Hazards

During my investigative journalism series regarding public health and environmental hazards in Jalisco, Mexico, one question that continued to rise to the top was corruption. In my research, I identified a superb expert: Dr. Jose Ivan Rodriguez-Sanchez. He is currently in residence at Rice University's James A. Baker III Institute for Public Policy – Mexico Center.

In December 2018, Mexico elected a new President: Andres Lopez Manuel Lobrador (aka AMLO). Lopez-Obrador has stated routinely he intends to eradicate corruption in Mexico. According to AMLO, the fiscal resources recovered from reductions in corruption in Mexico will serve to fund central aspects of his aggressive agenda to clean up Mexico's environment, and fund an array of other social programs. This interview delves into the plausibility of the new Mexican President's public pronouncements as they relate to corruption in Mexico.

The following is my interview with Dr. Rodriguez-Sanchez:

BIO: Excerpt from: **https://www.bakerinstitute.org/experts/jose-ivan-rodriguezsanchez/**

Jose Ivan Rodriguez-Sanchez, Ph.D., is the postdoctoral research fellow in international trade for the James A, Baker III Baker Institute Mexico Center. His research focuses on corruption in Mexico, international trade, migration, environmental economics and economic growth. Prior to joining the Baker Institute, he studied the energy and water markets of the Paso del Norte region as a research associate for the Hunt Institute at The University of Texas at El Paso. Rodriguez-Sanchez also worked as a deputy director in environmental economics at the Instituto Nacional de Ecología y Cambio Climático (INECC), where he analyzed different environmental problems in Mexico and crafted different public policy solutions. He has taught economics classes and seminars at the University of Colorado at Boulder, Instituto Tecnológico y de Estudios Superiores de Monterrey, Universidad Iberoamericana Puebla, Universidad de las Américas Puebla, Universidad Popular Autónoma del Estado de Puebla and Universidad Tecnológica de la Mixteca. His work has also been published in both academic and non-academic publications.

Rodriguez-Sanchez received a bachelor's degree in actuarial science and a master's degree in economics from the Universidad de las Américas Puebla, and master's and doctoral degrees in economics from the University of Colorado at Boulder, where he specialized in environmental economics, international trade and econometrics.

His most recent research and publications include:

- 09/13/2018 - Corruption in Mexico
- 12/11/2018 - Measuring Mexico's Corruption

The following is my interview with Dr. Rodriguez-Sanchez:

The Economic Consequences of Corruption in Mexico

1. My first question is: What led you to your current scholarly research and publication focus on the subject of Corruption in Mexico?

R: The economy of Mexico has not grown at the level needed to diminish major problems such as poverty, inequality, and crime in the last years. Hence, many Mexicans have had to migrate to the U.S.to improve their welfare. The economic growth of Mexico was approximately 2.5% during the presidency of Enrique Peña Nieto (2012-2018). This level of growth was not expected since many reforms and agreements were signed during his presidency that impaired GDP growth. One variable that could explain this low growth is corruption. Academia started to analyze this topic after major scandals of corruption in the public sector emerged to the media. However, this analysis is still in an initial stage and more work is needed. When I started working in the Mexico Center at the Baker Institute and after talking with Dr. Payan about this problem, I realized that we could analyze this topic to find the causes and consequences of corruption in Mexico from an economic perspective. Its definition and measurement are complex but doing that can help me to understand and provide efficient public policies that could diminish this problem in Mexico.

Mexico is one of the most corrupt countries in the world

2. In your publication, Measuring Mexico's Corruption (p.9/14), you state: "In 2017, Mexico scored 1.5 out of 6 and was ranked 126 out of 140 countries using the corruption component of the ICRG. Mexico dropped 25 places from 2012 to 2017, and it had high-to-moderate risk in its political risk rating, with a value close to 60.31 These figures coincide with the result given by the WBG for the CC. In 2017, Mexico scored 16 out of 100 on this indicator, and the WBG ranked it 175 out of 209 countries, which again indicates that Mexico is one of the most corrupt countries in the world. In order to combat corruption, prevent it from being systematized, and diminish its negative impact on Mexico's development, it is important to develop effective public policies." - My question is, in your opinion, can it

be reasonably stated that corruption is now systemic/systematized in Mexico? If not, why not?

R: There are different opinions on whether corruption is systemic in Mexico or not. In general, it seems that in Mexico corruption is a way to do business with the government. Corruption is in all levels of Mexican government and hence, it seems that corruption is systemic. I think this is almost the case, since corruption is not in all public officials and not all institutions are corrupt. However, if policy makers want to reduce corruption, it is necessary to face it with a systemic approach. Also, it is important to maintain the Rule of Law in Mexico, to have autonomous institutions, and free press to deter the problem of corruption. One key element in this systemic approach is the civil society. Society must continue to pressure Mexican government to punish corrupt acts and implement the National Anti-Corruption System. We have to keep in mind that all Mexicans are not corrupt, but we are the solution of it with correct public policies. Corruption affects the welfare of Mexicans in many ways, but we cannot allow corruption to become systemic in public and private sectors. So, we have to face corruption as if it were systemic, otherwise, corruption will infect the entire system and, in the end, it will be sure to be systemic.

Mexico's severe corruption problem has increased rapidly in recent years

3. You write: "Mexico has a severe corruption problem that has increased rapidly in recent years. Its international ranking has dropped dramatically in the last few years, and Mexico is now at the bottom in lists of corrupt countries in almost every international survey." (p.14 - Measuring) - My questions are: Why such an increase? What factors led to increasing corruption in such a short period of time in Mexico? Is measurement simply becoming better?

R. The problem of corruption in Mexico has increased rapidly in recent years due to major cases of corrupt acts such as Odebrecht, PEMEX, La Estafa Maestra, and diversion of public funds by former governors (e.g. Javier Duarte, Andres Granier, Roberto Borge). All these cases of corruption in the public and private sectors have affected the perception of corruption of Mexicans in the last years and hence, the indices that are based on it. A key factor that has increased this perception is impunity. During the presidency of Peña Nieto, all these cases went unpunished. The problem of corruption in Mexico has increased due to the high level of impunity. Unfortunately, the law does not apply in Mexico and corrupt acts are almost never punished. This impunity creates a system of corruption that can be diminished if corrupt acts are persecuted and punished.

To reduce corruption, we need to understand it better, and to achieve this reduction we must define corruption, and measure it more accurately. All these 1indices of perception of corruption has helped academia to understand and come up with better methodologies to measure corruption. Hence, these methodologies have improved in recent years, but still we must continue working on better methodologies for the perception of corruption and the actual level of corruption particularly in developing and poor countries.

Implementing Mexico's National Anti-Corruption System

4. In regard to developing (and implementing) effective public policies - The context for my question is this: According to multiple sources, "A landmark anti-corruption reform package that created a National Anti-Corruption System (Sistema Nacional Anticorrupción, SNA) and laid the foundation for a tougher and more comprehensive approach to combating corruption entered into force in July 2016."- Yet, this 2016 legislation has yet to be fully enacted in Mexico. My question is: Do you believe President AMLO's administration will implement this comprehensive legal framework, revitalize the confidence of the Mexican people to participate safely, and support the essential enforcement activities that must accompany it?

R. The president of Mexico, Andrés Manuel López Obrador, said in his first speech to the Congress that he is going to end corruption and impunity that prevent Mexico's rebirth. Indeed, the abatement of corruption in all levels of government is one of the objectives of his agenda. He pointed out that corruption can be dissuasive if he is honest and all other government workers emulate him. Unfortunately, he did not provide a specific plan to end corruption. Also, he sends confusing signals. He said that he will not punish corrupt acts that happened in the past, but for many years he accused people involved in corrupt acts of affecting Mexico. He has to obey the law and trust in the institutions that are in charge of overseeing the proper use of public funds and punish corrupt acts. The implementation of the SNA can provide AMLO with a high level of trust from Mexicans, since they promoted the development of this system. If he achieves to implement it with an autonomous prosecutor, the impact against corruption would be even greater. However, one problem is that the SNA needs public funds and up to now, AMLO has allocated less resources to key institutions that oversee the use and transparency of public resources. Hence, the implementation of the SNA could last longer, but if AMLO wants to end corruption, he should implement it as soon as possible.

The State of Measuring Corruption

5. As I read your most recent work about Measuring Corruption in Mexico, a quote from Former London School economist and social philosopher Charles Handy kept floating into my mind. Handy wrote: "The first step is to measure whatever can be easily counted. This is OK as far as it goes. The second step is to disregard that which can't be easily measured or to give it an arbitrary quantitative value. This is artificial and misleading. The third step is to presume that which can't be measured easily really isn't important. This is blindness. The fourth step is to say that which can't be easily measured really doesn't exist. This is suicide."2 My question is: How is this quote pertinent to the current state of measuring corruption in our world today?

R. Measuring corruption is very complex and measuring all corrupt acts in a society is a titanic task. However, institutions and academia must face this challenge and propose different and better approaches and methods to measure corruption. Corruption is present everywhere and acts as a contagious disease, but since it is under the surface, obtaining the number of corrupt acts and the costs of corruption to society is almost impossible. This does not mean that we cannot try to obtain these figures and improve methods, surveys, and indexes to measure corruption. It is worthwhile to face this challenge and inform society and the government about the seriousness of the problem of corruption in a city or a country. We have to start simple (e.g. one corrupt act) and then move to more complicated structures with the main objective to deter this problem that limits economic growth, development, and the welfare of people.

The Environment & Public Health – A Form of Corruption?

6. I have written extensively on the water supply and quality crisis in the Lerma-Chapala-Santiago basin. As the Lake Chapala situation relates to the Flint, Michigan debacle[3] in the U.S. it has been said that "In pure economic terms, it has been estimated that the economic costs of the Flint water debacle could exceed U.S. $300 billion.[4] It is incredibly expensive to ignore and/or mismanage burgeoning public health and environmental hazards; knowing that someone was going to get sick, someone was going to die...And sitting on the information.[5] My question is this: The current state of the Lake Chapala pollution is causing Chronic Kidney Disease (among other illnesses) and the primary source of water for millions in Guadalajara is distinctly imperiled. The Mexican people are getting sick, and in many documented cases, have become fatalities. Public officials in Mexico have been sitting on the information for years. How are the mismanagement of public funds related to the failure of public officials to address known public health and environmental hazards a legitimate form of corruption?

R. The mismanagement of public funds affects people related directly and indirectly to the basin in different ways. People cannot have the possibility to be protected against different diseases generated by this basin, since there are no resources to clean the water for human use. This mismanagement of public funds has a major economic impact. People who get sick cannot work and this generates a social cost and, in many cases, the government must pay this cost. This mismanagement generates a negative externality that diminishes the welfare of people. The government does not have to pay the cost of people getting sick, but the government must internalize this cost and let agents responsible for this cost pay for it. The fact that public funds are not used correctly, or not even used to clean the water or protect the environment causes a major problem for public health. In the end, this is another form of corruption, since the act of a public official does not guarantee the correct use of a public good.

Further Research

7. What are your next research endeavors regarding the subject of Corruption in Mexico?

R. The problem of corruption affects society in many ways and the causes and consequences of corruption have been discussed in recent years by academia. This discussion has been theoretical, and researchers have put it into practice and have measured the consequences of corruption and have found the causes of corruption in some countries using specific data from international surveys. However, in Mexico this analysis is scarce due to the limited data we have. The new surveys provide valuable information and using econometric it is possible to have a robust analysis of corruption. In my next research I will analyze the relationship of corruption and democracy in Mexico. It is expected that higher democracy leads to a lower perception of corruption controlling with other economic and socio-demographic variables. Other major research in my agenda is the estimation of the real cost of corruption in Mexico in the public sector. To achieve this, I must establish my definition of corruption and the corrupt acts involved in this definition and then the methodology to obtain it. This is important since AMLO has proposed that the end of corruption will provide his government with approximately 500,000 billion pesos (25 billion dollars). This latter figure is not based on a formal study; hence, it is a major duty to obtain a correct value of the cost of corruption in Mexico. Of course, other potential benefits of these research endeavors may arise when studies of this problem include the responsibility to inform society about the level of corruption and how to deter it.

Conclusion:

For Mexico in 2019, a significant, measurable reduction is corruption is essential to realize President Lopez-Obrador's agenda. How that might be accomplished remains uncertain, at best.

Special thanks to Dr. Jose Ivan Rodriguez-Sanchez and the James A. Baker III Institute for Public Policy – Mexico Center at Rice University.

CHAPTER NINE

Tourism and Public Safety in Mexico
Current Challenges in Jalisco, Mexico

Tourist Safety in Jalisco, Mexico

Mexico's Economic Tourism Engine

In 2016, travel & tourism provided 292 million jobs in worldwide, equivalent to 1 in 10 jobs. The industry generated US$7.6 trillion in worldwide revenue or 10.2% of worldwide GDP. In 2017 in Mexico, travel & tourism sustained 3,913,500 jobs (7.5% of total employment). Estimates expect this figure to rise by 3.2% in 2018 and by 2.3% to 5,051,000 jobs (8.5% of total employment) in 2028.1 The direct economic impact of travel & tourism to Mexico's GDP was MXN 3,506.1 bn (USD 185.4bn), 16.0% of GDP in 2017, It is forecast to increase by 3.0% in 2018, and 3.4% to MXN 5,041.9bn (USD 266.6bn), or 17.9% of GDP in 2028.2 According to the U.N. World Tourism Organization, in 2016, tourists crossing international boarders exceeded one billion for the first time. Estimates indicate cross-border international tourism visits will nearly double to 1.8 billion by 2030.3 Needless to say, this component of Mexico's economic engine is vital. It demands maintenance, investment and monitoring.

Yet, like any issue. there's a flip side to the upside potential of tourism for Mexico; environmental degradation, waste and water pollution, and perceived safety are three considerations prospective visitors take into account in their decision making processes. All three of these factors are current challenges in the Mexican state of Jalisco, where Guadalajara and Lake Chapala are located. This article examines this subject.

Risky Business

It's important to keep in mind that tourists travel to experience pleasure. Their unequivocal preference is to avoid risk, inconvenience, and potential threats to personal safety – and those factors that may diminish the enjoyment of their overall experience. In this sense, prospective tourists have a built-in risk avoidance mechanism.4 Countries and regions therein are acutely vulnerable to tourist perceptions of risk. Remember, an investment in or by an individual or group is discretionary. It is a human choice. Tourists can and do choose to substitute a less risky destination.

The perception of risk by tourists has been characterized as a *"major component of the decision-making process for evaluating destinations."*5 (2017 Osland et al). Tourist risks are the risks tourists typically contemplate in the preplanning stages before booking. Tourist risks are twofold; personal risk and destination risk. Personal risk is defined as prospective tourist perceptions of personal threats and experiences of the same during the planning stage of the proposed trip.6 (Tsaur, Tzeng, & Wang, 1997). Destination risk is the second dimension, defined as exposure to the likelihood of being victimized by crime, terrorism, disease, natural disasters, environmental hazards, and the absence of accessible, essential healthcare services.7 (Kozak, Crotts & Law, 2007).

Jalisco, Mexico: Perceptions of Risk by Prospective Tourists

Of course, every international traveler is familiar with the U.S. State Department Traveler Country Warning pronouncements.8 For Jalisco, the 28-12-2018 warning reads: **Jalisco state – Level 3: Reconsider Travel Reconsider travel due to crime.**

Violent crime and gang activity are common in parts of Jalisco state. In metropolitan Guadalajara, turf battles between criminal groups are taking place in areas frequented by U.S. citizens. Shooting incidents between criminal groups have injured or killed innocent bystanders. U.S. government employees may not travel to: Within 20 km (12 miles) of the Jalisco/Michoacán border, south of Route 120 , Highway 80 south of Cocula Highway 544 from Mascota to San Sebastian del Oeste. There are no restrictions on travel for U.S government employees to: Guadalajara Metropolitan Area, Riviera Nayarit (including Puerto Vallarta), Chapala, and Ajijic.

Crime in Jalisco

Nationally in Mexico, 65% of residents recently surveyed stated they view insecurity as the main problem in the country, while 79% view insecurity increasing in their states. One expert observes; "In terms of security, it is indisputable that the country is in "bankruptcy": crimes and victims on the rise, a policy of failed security and the discrediting of authorities and public institutions."9

In late November 2018, two explosive devices were thrown at the U.S. Embassy in Guadalajara. They exploded. There were no reported injuries. According to the Los Angeles Times; "This is an epoch of horror," former Gov. Sandoval acknowledged. But, he declared, the criminals "cannot be stronger than us. They cannot intimidate us." There were 247 homicides officially reported in Jalisco during the first two months of 2018, according to official statistics. That's an increase of 25% compared to the same time period in 2017 — which was a year that set a new record high for murders in the state of Jalisco and nationwide."10 In December 2018, a headline from the New York Post shouts "American Tourists Risk Death to Vacation in Mexico."11 Human rights activists declare disappearances also have increase to new highs in Jalisco, with more than 300 people reported missing in 2018. In December 2018, six state police officers were murdered in one incident. A 2018 article in Forbes declares: "more Americans were reported killed by homicide in Mexico than the combined total of Americans killed by homicide in every other country abroad." [12] Like I said, it's about perception.

The phrase "tourists of Mexico" is inhabited by a distinctly different and strategically important demographic to Mexico's tourism industry: Baby Boomers from North America relocating to Mexico for retirement. This cohort is looking to live (full or part-time) in Mexico. They are a group Mexico must be terribly effective in maintaining the attraction and addressing negative perceptions. Why?

Between 2016 and 2017, 2016-to 2017 Mexico was the unequivocal primary travel destination of choice for U.S. residents, rising 12% from 31 million to

35 million during those years alone.13 Interestingly enough, it has been noted that more U.S. residents are moving to Mexico than Mexicans moving to the U.S. 14 U.S. Baby Boomers are retiring – in droves. Some estimates suggest up to 10,000 a day.15 The number of U.S. citizens residing in Mexico ranges from 1.7 million to over 2 million.16 During the next decade, this figure is likely to grow significantly with the influx of retiring Baby Boomers from North America. Again, perception is everything. So is adaptation. Mexico must develop and adopt new, additional protective measures designed specifically for the preservation of the safety of tourists and English speaking retirees.

Digital Connectivity

Digital connectivity is essential to the tourism experience for those who travel from developed countries to Mexico. "The feeling of being able to connect is meaningful because a connectivity limitation might result in a negative travel experience."17 Mexico has work to do. In the Lake Chapala area, internet speeds are currently 3-5mbps. However, fiber optic cable is currently being installed. In Guadalajara, internet access is spotty, at best. As it relates to tourism, it is not solely the tourist who prioritizes digital connectivity; it includes the family, friends and colleagues of those tourists. Thus, the ability to text, call, and use on-line video mechanisms to communicate with "those at home" is paramount to the ability and necessity of tourists in Mexico to routinely confirm their safety to these audiences during their visits to Mexico. Again, substantial investment by the Mexican government is required to upgrade the current infrastructure in Jalisco to realize this necessity.

Environmental and Public Health Hazards

The environmental and public health hazards that inhabit the state of Jalisco have received international attention. The Lake Chapala Basin, a location central for tourism, expats, and vacationers is now well known for the environmental degradation and public health hazards that reside there.

The Lake Chapala basin is the most glaring example of the absence of meaningful and urgent Federal government intervention. Flows into the lake transport toxic sediments from the upper basin into the depths of the lake. Untreated sewage, run-off and wastewater are routinely discharged into the lake. Scientists have verified presence of heavy metals in humans, fish, foods and flora are apparent. Municipalities cannot afford the electricity required to operate sewage and wastewater treatment plants. The lake is infested by water hyacinths and other invasive species. The incidences of Chronic Kidney disease in communities that reside along the lake shore remain the 2nd worst in the world. In some locations around the lake (indigenous communities), the incidence of CKD is 3-5 times greater than any other place on the planet. Need I say more? The Mexican National Government must designate the Lake Chapala Basin as a NaturALMO site – whereby the Federal government has yet to initiate the essential comprehensive, multi-faceted strategy to intervene in this degraded environment – and rehabilitate and restore this national treasure.

Points to Ponder: Risk Management Considerations for the Mexican Tourism Industry in Jalisco, Mexico

"Enrique de la Madrid, Mexico's former Secretary of Tourism, said during a press conference in May 2018 that "crime rates in some parts of the country have been increasing" and the Mexico Tourism Board plans to add additional emphasis on the safety narrative; "We're working on a campaign for the U.S. to stress that violence hasn't impacted tourists," he stated."[18] (The current Secretary of Tourism in the Lopez-Obrador administration is Miguel Torruco Marqués). As an example, in Acapulco, local government has established a Tourist Assistance and Protection Center — aka CAPTA. This is a service where foreign tourists can report experiences and obtain assistance if they are victims of a crime."[19] According to OSAC, "Tourism Police are specifically assigned to police tourist areas and are commonly the only units that speak English. Their main purpose is to enhance the safety of tourist areas by deterring crime and responding to accidents. Tourist police are not able to take *denuncias* but can assist travelers in contacting the authorities who can."[20]

The same is required in Guadalajara and Ajijic. Recently, one cell phone was provided by the local newspaper (Lake Chapala Reporter) to local law enforcement in Chapala so English speaking residents can call to report crime and request assistance.

Mexico's Secretariat of Tourism Miguel Torruco Marqués should consider the following to further insure the safety of tourists, expats and the like in Mexico:

- Establish a national hotline for tourists to call to report crime, threats to safety and request assistance. This mechanism should be staffed 24/7/365 and provide multiple incoming lines with English speaking/bi-lingual operators who can facilitate the assistance required – with local Mexican law enforcement agencies throughout the country.

- Establish, train and staff additional CAPTA deployments in high density tourist meccas (in Jalisco - Zona Centro Historico and Ajijic are obvious priorities). These CAPTA deployments may be seasonal, commensurate with high tourist seasons.

- National tourist assistance hotline phone numbers should be posted, numerous, and be highly prominent in locations frequented by tourists in Jalisco.

- Mexico's Secretariat of Tourism must leverage technology to more effectively manage prospective tourist perceptions – that are currently heavily influenced by the headlines of mainstream media focused on the most heinous acts that threaten public safety and public health.

- Tourism promotion is typically directed outward from a country to attract prospective visitors. However, as evidenced by the degradation in the Lake Chapala basin, Mexico's Secretariat of Tourism Miguel Torruco Marqués must advocate *internally* insuring the Federal government initiates the essential comprehensive, multi-faceted strategy to intervene in this degraded environment – and rehabilitate and restore this national treasure. He must also advocate for connectivity technology upgrades that tourists require – and impact their experiences and perceptions.

Conclusions

Tourism is a strategically imperative component of Mexico's current economy – and its' future. It is also fragile and subject to a myriad of influences. Mexico must direct additional investments in the care, preservation, enhancement and technological improvements of the tourist experience. All must be designed to protect and invigorate the ongoing growth in this component of Mexico's economy. It is essential. Internet access is ubiquitous in our world. Tourist evaluations of Mexico as their destination are influenced by the perceptions of public safety, connectivity and environmental and public health hazards. The perception of Jalisco, Mexico is currently problematic. An immediate, concerted effort is required to address this reality. May Mexico's new Secretariat of Tourism Miguel Torruco Marqués lead the mission. Jalisco's new Governor Enrique Alfaro Ramírez should also be intimately involved in this effort.

CHAPTER TEN

Lake Chapala Proposed Development

Progress? Perplexing? Perilous or Preposterous

Progress?

"The Lakeside area has become a dreamscape for developers. Local governments tend to lack long-term vision to implement wise policies and strategies to manage inevitable urban sprawl, often bending the rules to cater to investors on the premise that economic benefits outweigh the downsides of unchecked growth."[1] So states one area news outlet, which has delivered some excellent reporting on the prospective, mind-bending scale of development planned for the Lake Chapala area.

A current resident of Ajijic says:

"AMLO (The New Mexican President Andres Manuel Lopez-Obrador) wants to turn this area into a tourist mecca but it is going to require massive investments in infrastructure. I live in Riberas and the power goes out for days on end. There is no sewage treatment plant here despite Riberas being the largest community in Lake Chapala. The water quality is questionable and the internet service is pathetic. From cleaning up the lake to improving the infrastructure it's going to take a lot of money that the government doesn't have. The municipal Lake Chapala government is broke. The electrical grid is a disaster. The north shore is beyond congested. The carettera is a disaster and there's no way it can handle the existing traffic, let alone an increase in population."[2]

According to the Lake Chapala Reporter,[3] The Institute of Pensions of the State of Jalisco (IPEJAL) intends to invest 390 million pesos ($US 20 million) as a member of a group of investors who intend to build a city of 17,000 residents (more than current population of Ajijic). It is to be located in the area of Santa Cruz de la Soledad and San Nicolas de Ibarra (which are under the jurisdiction of the municipality of Chapala). A development company named Santa Cruz Immobiliaria de Chapala SA de CV has obtained title to 275 hectares (680 acres) out of the required 450 hectares (1,112 acres). The plan is to construct 3,066 single family homes, 812 duplexes, and 396 assisted living units. The plans also include a hotel, shopping center, medical clinics, a golf course, etc. A Madrid attorney, Manuel Ramon de Asis Orta of Covasis S de R de CV (a limited liability variable stock corporation) – is a representative and legal attaché of a another member of the group. He is the main contact for the group to AIPROMADES - who is responsible for completing the required environmental impact studies. Another shareholder is the Metromexa agency ... a very large auto and auto parts dealer/distributor in Mexico.4

Research by investigative journalist Manuel Jacobo revealed "the acquisition of land goes back to 2009, accomplished through political manipulation and intimidation of the ejido community of communal land owners in Santa Cruz."5 These tactics were purportedly facilitated by former local government officials in Chapala, and a number of state agencies.6

There is another residential housing development planned for the area above Las Brisas, across from the existing Chapala Haciendas development. This development is estimated at 75 acres (30 hectares).

This development proposal has led to the formation of an opposition group based in Ajijic, called Chimalli Axixic. This group is "comprised of Lakeside Mexicans and members of the expat community. It is our call "to shield" the hillside above Ajijic from further development."7 They are raising funds to retain legal counsel to fight the proposed development above Ajijic: "Chimalli Axixic is a non-profit, non-partisan social organization that promotes the care of the environment in the town of Ajijic and other towns along the Lake Chapala shore; It also aims to raise awareness among society and government entities at all levels (municipal, state and federal) to prioritize the promotion and care of natural areas."8 Local Realtors have been reported to be attempting to sell some parcels. Needless to say, the current ecosystem will be indelibly transformed should the planned development emerge into a reality.

Perilous and Perplexing

Incompetence, mismanagement and corruption inhabit the machinery of governance in Chapala. In January 2019, raw sewage is leaking onto the streets of San Antonio Tlayacapan, moving toward Lake Chapala.9 In December 2018, the Chapala Municipal Planning and Urban Development Department identified 100 construction projects that have licenses without the requisite land use and technical permitting.10 In the same month, it was revealed that the land use designation was changed in March 2018 for the Tepalo Hills plat above Ajijic - from protected to residential.11 December 2018 continued to rain bad news for Chapala when Chapala City Hall faced seizure of its assets by virtue of an unpaid 4 million peso debt to an auto parts supplier.12 The contractor for garbage collection has removed two trucks from service as part of an effort to exert pressure on Chapala to pay up on a past due debt of 6 million pesos for their past work.13 The deluge of unconscionable continued for Chapala with the revelation that the Comptroller's Office of Chapala notified 28 people from the previous administration of "irregularities." In Chapala's Public Works Department these maladies total in excess of 5 million pesos in missing funds without verifiable receipts for expenditures on projects.14 This figure did not include the value for 7 vehicles missing during the transition between administrations – including several garbage trucks.15

October and November 2018 weren't any prettier for the municipality of Chapala. A report from ITESO noted that Lake Chapala's waters contain high levels of fecal coliforms and levels of arsenic at levels above WHO safety standards.16 The Latin American Water Tribunal held a court hearing regarding Lake Chapala and rendered a stunning, negative verdict. Later in October, lack of a water treatment facility in Riberas del Pilar (and heavy rains) led to septic tank overflows contaminating groundwater for residents and animals.17 In November, it was reported that the municipality of Chapala had not paid for waste water treatment in 3 years and owes the State Water Commission (CEA) 6 million pesos.18 It is also seeking a loan of 14 million pesos to pay the back wages of City workers.19 Around Thanksgiving 2018, overflows of dirty water in Ajijic and Chapala became apparent. Due to the pressure exerted by the high lake water levels, the drainage systems in both cities suffered damage. The drainage system in Chapala must be completely replaced.20

With the clearly established inability to manage the current permitting processes for development and construction and municipal governance in a remotely effective manner – well – the future for this area appears tangibly and legitimately perilous and perplexing.

Preposterous

The current infrastructure of the *existing* area requires replacement and monumental investments. This includes water supply, water quality, water distribution, sewage and waste water treatment, storm run-off systems, digital connectivity enhancements, the power grid, and garbage collection and disposal – and – we haven't even got to traffic and roads yet. Oh, I'm sorry; did I fail to mention the urgent need to intervene comprehensively to clean up the scientifically established, public health and environmental hazards that currently inhabit the Lake Chapala basin? (The Lerma and Santiago Rivers are duly noted).

Current residents of Ajijic have reverted to admonishing prospective residents to "move on," as the existing area cannot accommodate ongoing growth. We need to *hear* these voices and seriously consider the meaning they are attempting to convey. These voices recognize "what was isn't anymore." Growth groans. You can see it, hear it and smell it everywhere around Lakeside.

Conclusions:

One observer concludes: "Considering the impact on the area's flora, fauna and natural resources, not to mention quality of life for people, it all paints a grim picture for the future of an area once prized for its quiet, rural setting."[21]

When building a subdivision, region, country or home, a fundamental consideration is a stable foundation, and the infrastructure it stands on. Before you build onto an existing structure, it's best to examine the structural integrity of what you are attaching your planned expansion to.

In the rush for the wealthy to deploy capital and build expansive new developments for outsiders to enjoy, the challenge at present in the Lakeside/Chapala area is to hit the pause button. The existing infrastructure needs replacement, substantive upgrades, and a likely nine figure Mexican federal government investment – overseen by a newly designated federal authority where the responsibility and accountability for producing the desired results resides.

The "way it was" is now a memory for the current residents of Lakeside. There's no going back. Yet, the way ahead must be tangibly influenced by those whose voices speak for the voiceless; flora, fauna, natural resource preservation and restoration, and the victims of manipulation and corruption.

Preposterous?

CHAPTER ELEVEN

Is Lake Chapala Polluted?

I have received a number of questions about the nature and degree of the pollution in Lake Chapala, originating from the recent series of articles I authored on this subject. I am a journalist, not a scientist. However, I am trained to sift through mountains of information to identify themes, strengths and weakness – as well as the essence of what the data indicates.

It must be noted that the environmental and public health hazards resident in the Lake Chapala basin are well researched and well documented by scientific research from a number of disciplines. Most of this is available via internet search engines. Some is not. I acquired and reviewed both. I also interviewed public health, environmental, and other professionals directly involved in the endeavors of investigating the environmental and public health hazards that inhabit the Lake Chapala basin.

I posted an article about the transcript of the Latin American Water Council proceedings held in Guadalajara, Mexico. The genesis for much of the testimony that was provided during this court hearing came from this study: Institute of Technology and Higher Studies of the West (ITESO). In my opinion, this is one of the best studies because of the data set was longitudinal (2012-2018) and conducted by a team of very well regarded researchers. **I discuss this particular study here:**

2018-08: Quality Data Analysis Report: Department of Mathematics and Physics. The title of the research endeavor is: Report of Water Quality Data Analysis of Lake Chapala. Tlaquepaque, Jalisco: ITESO. It was published December 2018.

The authors of this study are: Sánchez-Torres, Juan D .; Nuño-Sánchez, Saúl A .; Martinez-Alvarado, Juan C .; Ruiz-Cruz, Riemann Sánchez-Torres, J.D .; Nuño-Sánchez, S.A .; Martínez-Alvarado, J.C. and Ruiz-Cruz.

A team composed by Dr. Carlos Peralta, Lic., Loreto Irene Soto Rivas and Ing, Ana Sofia Macías Ascanio, Department of Sociopolitical and Legal Studies (DSOJ) of ITESO,) made a public records request to the Mexican Federal government. The information obtained by this team was via a request for transparency on March 2, 2018 to the National Water Commission with the via folio number 1610100154118. This petition requested all the information that they (The National Water Commission) possessed related to the water quality of Lake Chapala. This team also prepared the formal complaint that was presented to the Latin American Water Tribunal at ITESO (Jesuit University of Guadalajara) October 22-26 2018. You can read the formal complaint and the outcome of these proceedings **HERE**.

The National Water Commission in Mexico is known as CONAGUA. (Comisión Nacional del Agua). It is an agency within the Mexican Federal government that acts as an administrative and technical advisory commission to Mexico's Ministry of the Environment and Natural Resources (aka SEMARNAT). CONAGUA manages the nation's waters, hydrological system, and engages in social development activities. A database was created by the ITESO team of researchers and CONAGUA based upon the information they received from CONAGUA. This database contains information generated by CONAGUA about the presence of various elements detected in lake water samples obtained in some 34 monitoring stations located at different geographical locations around Lake Chapala. The chronology of this data was from November 21, 2012 to February 8, 2018.

The research team from ITESO selected only certain, specific elements contained in the database, which include: "Arsenic, Fecal Coliforms, Chromium, Biochemical Oxygen Demand (BOD), Chemical Demand of Oxygen (COD), Escherichia Coli, Mercury, Ammoniacal Nitrogen, Nitrates, Nitrites, Nitrogen Organic, Total Nitrogen, Orthophosphate, Phosphorus, Lead, pH, Total Dissolved Solids (TDS) and Solids Total Suspended (SST)."

<u>Here are excerpts BELOW</u> (quotes – translated to English) from the ITESO report (emphasis is mine):

The results of the present analysis showed that the monitoring stations, in general, have obtained higher than average concentrations are located throughout all the periphery of the Lake. It also realizes that all parameters, except Lead they have been detected in all the monitoring stations.

Arsenic: The samplings show that in Lake of Chapala, Arsenic has been detected.

Fecal Coliforms: It is necessary to indicate that Fecal Coliforms are from sewage discharges, as the name implies, come from the feces Fecal. In this regard, the NOM-127-SSA1-1996 and the WHO, specify that for water to be good quality there should not be a presence of these microorganisms. However, it is clear that there is presence of these in the Lake of Chapala, *indicating that the water of Lake Chapala, in itself, is not drinkable.*

UNTREATED WASTEWATER: IT IS EVIDENT THAT UNTREATED WASTEWATER DISCHARGES ARE BEING MADE TO LAKE CHAPALA, AND THAT IN ADDITION, IN RELATION TO THIS PRIORITY PARAMETER, LIFE IS NOT BEING PROTECTED.

Fecal Coliforms: All the stations have maintained, on average, a concentration that exceeds-by far-what is established according to NOM-001-SEMARNAT-1994. In that meaning it can be interpreted that:

LAKE CHAPALA DOES NOT MEET ANY OF THE STANDARDS THAT PROTECT THE HEALTH OF BOTH PEOPLE AND ECOSYSTEMS, IN RELATION TO THE PARAMETER PRIORITY OF FECAL COLIFORMS (COLI_FEC).

Aquatic Life: It is known that all stations maintain concentrations above the reference of Standard 001 that protects aquatic life.

Polluted: The overall average of all measurements is 46.92 mg / L, *which indicates the Lake is "Polluted"*(Concentrations of Chemical Oxygen Demand obtained during the measurement period). "COD" measures organic matter caused by industrial residual water discharges. In that sense, this parameter officially relates water quality to industrial water discharges, and serves to indicate how affected the water of the lake is – by the aqueous waste of the industries with which it has some connection.

The stations located within Lake Chapala show high concentrations.

Phosphorous: It is important to mention that the presence of Phosphorus in the water propitiates eutrophication phenomenon, which is considered as a problem of pollution by the alterations to the balance and to the dynamics of flora and fauna that have Lake Chapala as an ecosystem.

E Coli: The Fecal Coliform (COLLI_FEC) and Escherichia Coli (E_COLI) parameters are very much above the maximum allowed value, that is to say they violate by far the NOM-127-SSA1-1994 and in that meaning it can be said:

THE WATER OF LAKE CHAPALA HAS CONTAINED FECAL COLIFORMS, AND IN SPECIAL E-COLI IN CONCENTRATIONS*THAT MAY POSE A HEALTH RISK AND THAT SHOULD TO BE SERVED WITH WATER TREATMENT PROCESSES PRIOR TO DISTRIBUTION IN THE SUPPLY NETWORK.*

These averages show that *Lake Chapala has Fecal Coliforms in very high concentrations superior to all reference standards*.

E Coli: According national and international references, for water to be potable it must not have presence of Escherichia Coli, in addition, wastewater discharges must have a concentration of 1000 NMP / 100mL to protect aquatic life, according to Standard 001. In this sense, with the global average has the approximation that *the water of Chapala Lake per se is not potable*, and it needs a purifying process to eliminate these bacteria, because they are pathogenic. **It is known that all stations maintain concentrations above the reference of Standard 001 that protects aquatic life.**

The above does not address the bodies of research on the contamination of aquatic species, avian species, ecosystem degradation, and the research documenting Chronic Kidney Disease among primarily indigenous populations that reside around the lake.

I hope this article helps those who have sent inquiries to me. I cannot reveal the source that provided with me with this research paper, prior to its public release.

Chapter TWELVE

Corruption in Mexico – An Environmental and Public Health Hazard Perspective

Abstract:

In this analysis I examine specific environmental and public health hazards in the Lake Chapala basin in Jalisco, Mexico as a consequence of corruption in Mexico. As elements of this examination, we address the state of measuring corruption in society. We also review the data regarding the presence of corruption in Mexico at present. Next, we analyze how environmental and public health hazards are legitimate consequences of corruption. We address how the recent political changes in Mexico represent the opportunity to implement the effective policy, financing and regulatory framework to more effectively interrupt the sources of corruption that have fed the depth, breadth and current state of this specific array of ongoing, unaddressed, environmental and public health hazards. Finally we propose policy considerations to intervene, rehabilitate, and restore Lake Chapala as a critical source of water for millions of residents of Guadalajara and the surrounding area in the State of Jalisco. This work product is testament to the necessity for journalists who can be trained along with civil society organizations to present the consequences of corrupt acts on the human right to water and sanitation.

Disclaimer:

Research Methods

The purpose of this analysis is to identify the relationship between environmental and public health hazards in a specific geographic location in Jalisco, Mexico as outcomes of corruption in Mexico. This study used secondary data analysis/content analysis of materials published in the scientific literature (both the physical and social sciences), reports of numerous commissions, governmental agencies, advocacy groups, and media publications. The criteria used to select these materials were: the theoretical and empirical pertinence of the research, and the validity of observations and conclusions. The primary research methods are content analysis and synthesis as a method of studying the relationship between environmental and public health hazards in Jalisco, Mexico as outcomes of corruption in Mexico. The theoretical framework used as a basis for the interpretation of the results is descriptive and analytical research methodology. This paper also includes observational data obtained by four weeks on-site in the Guadalajara and Lake Chapala areas. This included interviews with residents, public officials, visitors, journalists and members of advocacy and regulatory groups.

<u>Case Study</u>: Student Engagement - Public Education – Advocacy Content

This is a case study. It is designed as a public education tool, content and reference for advocacy groups and government entities, and a vehicle to engage students in enhancing critical, thinking, research, and communication skills when analyzing and evaluating complex, multi-dimensional, real life situations. This specific case study is designed to inspire critical thinking. From a public education and advocacy perspective, it is constructed to engender motivation to move from passive observation to active advocacy involvement. It is crafted to be shared.

Locus:

The Locus for this endeavor is Lake Chapala, Mexico. It is located in what is often referred to as the Lerma-Chapala basin. In terms of the North American continent, Mexico encompasses 1.94 million km2 (750,563 square miles). Mexico currently has a population exceeding 131 million, growing at 1.3% per annum.1 79% of the population resides in urban environments (103,527,244 people). The median age in Mexico is 27.9 years. Politically, Mexico is divided into 32 federal entities. One is a federal district, which includes Mexico City, and 31 are states. Each state has its own elected government. For 2018, the national budget of Mexico was 5.28 trillion pesos (US $276.98 billion). 2

Lake Chapala is the largest natural water reservoir in Mexico. It is the third largest freshwater lake in Latin America. It is the second highest in altitude in the America's at an altitude of 1524 m above sea level. Located in the western-central part of Mexico, its' locus is found at 102° 40'45" n 103° 25'30" longitude west and 20° 07' and 20° 21' latitude north. The surface area of the lake is 1146.7 km. Median depth ranges from 8-16m (seasonally dependent). This body of water is shared between the states of Michoacan (14%) and Jalisco (86%). The Lerma-Chapala basin is considered the most important in Mexico.3 The Lerma-Chapala basin includes portions of the states of Guanajuato, Jalisco, Mexico, Michoacan and Queretaro. The ecosystem and water resources are managed by a mosaic of agencies domiciled in all three levels of government; federal, state and municipal. Management of the country's hydrological system, its administration, and technical advisory capacity is the purview of The National Water Commission (CONAGUA – established 1989) - in the Ministry of the Environment and Natural Resources (SEMARNAT). There are also a network of state cater commissions (Comisiones Estatales del Agua – CEAs), and municipal water authorities and basin councils. In November 2018, Mexico's committee on water resources, drinking water and sanitation approved a proposed 95% annual increase to Conagua's 2019 budget to MXN52.5 billion pesos ($2.59 billion).4

The Lerma River flows into Lake Chapala. The river is 750 km (466 miles) in length. It originates at an altitude above 3,000 meters (over 9,500 feet) above sea level in Mexico's central high plateau. The Lerma River is considered as one of the most polluted rivers in Mexico.5 Throughout its journey, the river in compromised by untreated discharges from chemical, textile, and manufacturing industries. Other pollutants include livestock related industries and agriculture. Other than precipitation, the Lerma River is the main water inflow for Lake Chapala. Pollutants are deposited into the lake after a rainfall. Rainfall in the basin averages 29 inches or 735mm per year. Untreated wastewater, storm water and sewage are also discharged directly into both the river and the lake. The outflow of the lake is via the Santiago River. It flows to the Pacific Ocean.

Lake Chapala is the primary source of water for Guadalajara, the second largest city in Mexico. The greater Guadalajara area is home for an estimated 5+ million residents. Lake Chapala, as a future source of water for Guadalajara has been characterized as both uncertain and unsustainable. As a pair of recent researchers conclude: "it will be difficult to continue to use the lake as the main source of freshwater for the Guadalajara metropolitan area without substantial interventions."[6]

The Corruption Challenge:

You confront corruption by holding people accountable for both actions and in actions. This is as true for known public health and environmental hazards, as it is for commonly referred to forms of corruption where bribery, money laundering, nepotism, illegal enrichment. Extortion, electoral fraud, embezzlement, deception/dishonesty for gain, influence peddling and misappropriation flourish. It's not as simple as it sounds.

Needless to say, a *universally* accepted definition of corruption, and a method to measure it accurately, is difficult, if not impossible.[7] Researchers continue to make progress in this arena. The social phenomenon of corruption is comprised of many elements, which require different definitions and measurement techniques to capture. As one study observes; "From a scholarly perspective, the challenge remains to deal with noisy data that try to capture behavior that is hidden from plain sight."[8]

However, its costs are even more difficult to pin down. As one moves from attempting to monetize the cost of the more visible forms of corruption (embezzlement for example), to the less visible (public health and environmental hazards), the task becomes even more challenging.

This article focuses on the country of Mexico, water, and the largest body of freshwater in the country – Lake Chapala. Without water, human life cannot be sustained. With corruption, the sources, quality, access, delivery and management/rehabilitation of the same is imperiled further. As the Water Integrity Outlook states: "Water is vital for life: the life of every human being on this planet and the life of the planet itself. However, despite international legislation over many decades, access to safe, clean and adequate water supply and sanitation services is still not available to all."9 Mexico is a current day example of this reality.

One of the reasons for this measurement challenge is the void in the body of social research on the subject of the causes and consequences of corruption.10 The current body of social research on corruption in society is heavily weighted to the results and analysis of survey research. These studies focus primarily on both the perceptions and experiences of people with corruption. Of course, perception is impacted by experience. Perception is also affected by an array of other variables including employment status, occupation, age, gender, education, income, inequality, religion, and truthfulness of respondents to uncomfortable corruption study questions.11 Like any other subject that is difficult to define and measure, the current state of our aptitude regarding the prevention, detection, reduction of corruption via public policy remains evolving.

The Downstream Dilemma

It is important to note that the reality of environmental and public health hazards as legitimate outcomes of corruption reside *downstream* from the primary reservoir of social research on corruption. National scandals, bribery, influence peddling, and the primary government contract granting apparatus are located in densely populated urban centers. This is also the location of the vast majority of mainstream media resources. It is the locus of country political power. In Latin America, upward of 80 percent of the population live in cities. Strategically important resources of water are typically located substantial distances from these locales, and may not be sources of water for the populations that reside in capital cities of countries. Furthermore, the regulatory repositories for corruption reporting are also primarily domiciled in the urban centers of political power. Such is the reality in Mexico – and the critically important national water resource of Lake Chapala.

Public perception of corruption in societies is deeply influenced by the impact of media. The lack of access to mainstream media is so noted as it relates to the impoverished. Historically, mainstream media attention focuses on corruption scandals involving primarily national governments and high ranking officials. "Unfortunately, in focusing on national-level corruption, the media, government, and the general public have missed the equally important story of local corruption."[12] Thus, from a media influence standpoint, public perceptions of corruption are contorted by the same. This deflects attention toward the existence, locus, nature and degree of other multi-dimensional forms that exist in a society. Furthermore, the ineffective and unjust handling of the prosecution of those involved in national corruption scandals broadly erodes public confidence.

This **mainstream media focus** on scandalous, national incidents of corruption has an unintended consequence of creating social distance between the citizenry and their government officials. It eviscerates public trust with citizens who experience other forms of corruption in their daily lives – whose confidence is fundamental in becoming/being participants in a system that detects reports and regulates corruption in any society. It also obscures the fact that corruption is institutionalized and systematized in a society versus the media promoted characterization of corruption as a scandalous national malfeasance incidence characterization. National media attention on corruption characterized as incidental, national, and as scandalous mutes the importance of the *experience* of systemic corruption in their daily lives.

In this sense, national media attention to national corruption scandals diverts attention away from the reality of the environmental and public health hazards that confront the local citizenry - where they live – downstream from the centers of power in a nation. It is disempowering. It obscures the face of the millions of people who actually suffer on a day-to-day basis from corruption. This is particularly true in developing countries where the human right to water and effective sanitation services are concerned.

A note of recognition is appropriate here. In Latin American countries it is **risky business to be a journalist.** This is acutely true regarding investigations of corruption associated with environmental degradation and public health. One quote seems to sum up this reality: "Journalists also constitute one of the main groups at risk in Mexico. According to the statistics, Mexico has become one of the most dangerous countries for journalists. Between 2000 and 2016, at least 120 journalists were killed mostly in the states of Veracruz, Oaxaca, Tamaulipas, Guerrero and

Chihuahua. They may face violence during the coverage of protests, threatened by the organized crime or harassed by authorities, when they investigate stories related to corruption."13 One might believe this quote is pertinent only to cases involving the illicit narcotics business. It's not. Other observers point not: "The world is deadlier than ever for land and environmental defenders, with agribusiness the industry most linked to killings. It has never been a deadlier time to defend one's community, way of life, or environment. Our latest annual data into violence against land and environmental defenders shows a rise in the number of women and men killed last year to 207 - the highest total we have ever recorded."14 According to the Mexican Center for Environmental Law (aka CEMDA), not even one of the 15 murders of environmentalists in 2017 has been solved.15

As one moves away from the locus of political power, another problematic reality raises its head; income inequality. According to the OECD, Mexico has the second greatest income inequality (for member countries – after Chile).16 It is here, in the more rural regions of Mexico, where Lake Chapala resides. The area is inhabited by numerous indigenous populations (among others); people who have depended upon the quality of the water in the lake for their survival. They use these waters – as they have for generations - for drinking, cooking, harvesting fish stocks, and irrigation for agricultural products. For the impoverished, and those struggling with subsistence living, dependent upon the quality of the waters in Lake Chapala, both the current reality - and the prospects for the future - is startling. Research has documented that the level of corruption increases due to income inequality. The poor are more vulnerable to numerous forms of corruption and hampered to hold those who perpetrate corruption accountable. Inequality promotes the tolerance corruption as acceptable behavior.17 One should not overlook the impact of fear and powerlessness as a consequence of corruption. Furthermore, the willingness of these victims of corruption, and their inputs into studies of corruption in their lives becomes diminished, as one moves downstream and out into more rural areas from the dominions of densely populated, urban, in-country political power.

Granted, environmental and public health hazards as outcomes of corruption are multi-faceted. I am not overlooking the fact that these outcomes are also caused and reside where the extraction and overexploitation of natural resources is domiciled (mining and logging sites for example). Yet, strategically essential reservoirs of drinking water, like

Lake Chapala, are located downstream from the primary tributaries that contribute mightily to their degradation.

Thus, research on the more intangible outcomes of corruption like the presence, form and costs of current, widely recognized environmental and public health hazards has become a tertiary subject for study by scholars' vis-à-vis the totality of the research completed in this subject area. However, it must be noted that environmental advocacy groups, the OECD, WHO, UN, WB, as well as NGO's and independent journalists have made outstanding contributions to our knowledge base regarding the relationship between environmental degradation, public health, and corruption.

It's important to note the difference between the physical and social sciences, as it relates to calculating the costs of social phenomena like corruption. Remember, oceanography is a physical science. It is built upon the time tested principles of the scientific method and the disciplines of mathematics, physics, astronomy, chemistry, geography, biology, seismology and the like. We have developed tools to accurately measure the physical properties of earthly elements like water. An example would be a simple salinity test. These tests are widely utilized, standardized and the results from one test to the next can be compared along with their methodological procedures.

Economics is a social science. It is a relatively recent, inter-disciplinary human construct - an expression/application of the amalgamation of tools, methods and elements of other disciplines - used to attribute symbols, narratives, value, standardized constructs, perception, understanding and meaning in the economic realm of human activities. According to Andrew W. Lo - the Charles E. and Susan T. Harris Professor at the MIT Sloan School of Management and director of the MIT Laboratory for Financial Engineering, "The economics profession suffers from a psychological condition best described as "physics envy."[18]

As it relates to the measurement of the costs of corruption, this distinction between social research and economics as developing disciplines in the social sciences and the more established disciplines in the physical sciences cannot be understated. One must appreciate that economics is "simply another tool to examine the human experience."[19] It is also a very nascent one; "The first treatise on economics published in this country was Daniel

Ra Raymond's Thoughts on Political Economy in 1820 (expanded into Elements of Political Economy in 1823)."[20] The eminent economist John Kenneth Galbraith once wrote about his field of inquiry: "The cost of believing in equilibrium — of seeing the study of economics as a search for improved knowledge of a fixed and final subject matter and thus as a hard science like physics or chemistry — is to be in an ineluctable march to obsolescence."[21] Thus, in attributing economic costs to social phenomenon like corruption, we remain in the process of developing more effective tools. Yet, the current state of our measurement capability remains enslaved to the inertia of applying the currently available measures to this quantitative reality.

Finally, we currently *attribute* costs to social phenomena like corruption. Our attributions (in the most reliable cases) are accompanied by disclosures of our methods, assumptions, calculations, and limitations of said socio-economic reality. To be fair, my remarks above are not limited to the subject area of measuring the presence, form and economic value of corruption in society. On the contrary, the same is true for a whole host of social phenomena like drug abuse, crime, environmental degradation of water resources, and the public health costs associated therewith. However, the reality of corruption in society as a multi-dimensional form of crime, it is most typically conducted opaquely, outside the view and established mechanisms of public and regulatory detection.

In terms of calculating the costs of corruption globally, estimates vary widely. According to a December 2018 United Nations estimate, corruption costs five percent of global GDP or U.S. 2.3 trillion dollars – *annually*.22 The U.N. also recognizes that corruption "*strips nations of their natural resources*."23 Public health and environmental hazards remain tangible outcomes of corruption whose measurements, causes, consequences and costs are typically avoided by corruption scholars. This reality is acutely apparent in Mexico. This article examines this subject.

Mexico's Corruption Reality:

Enter Mexico. In July 2018, Mexican voters cast ballots for approximately 2,800 elected positions at the state and local level, 9 governors, a new Congress at the federal level, and a new president for their nation.24 President Andres Manuel Lopez Obrador (aka AMLO) assumed office in

December 2018. Part of AMLO's platform is called NaturAMLO – his promise to clean up Mexico's environment. According to AMLO, taxes won't increase, Mexico will not incur more debt, and the price of food will remain stable. Where will the money come from to realize AMLO's agenda? The theoretical source of funding will arise in part, due to an overall reduction of corruption in Mexico.25 This suggestion by the AMLO administration is not without a basis in social scientific studies; "Cross-country research suggests that the gains from reducing corruption and improving governance are large."26

Mexico is no exception to the economic drain of corruption. According to a study completed by the World Economic Forum, corruption is viewed by Mexican citizens as *one of the most important issues facing the country, second only to insecurity.*"27 The WEF's *Global Competitiveness Report* stated that "Mexico's weakest link is its institutions, and corruption is the most problematic factor for doing business. This presents a significant barrier to social stability and economic growth."28 A startling observation confirms the economic drain on the Mexican economy: "Mexican households spent 14% of their income on "mordidas," and households earning the minimum wage spent 33%, demonstrating that corruption acts as a regressive tax for the poor."29 Other attempts to calculate the cost of corruption in Mexico range from 2% to 10% of Mexico's GDP.30 In 2017, Mexico's GDP was U.S. $1.15 trillion dollars.31 It is important to note that the calculation of any country's GDP does not include the costs of either natural resource extraction and/or their degradation.

The OECD has estimated the annual economic cost of water pollution in Mexico at US$6 billion per year. In 2017, The OECD observed; "Mexico needs to increase the financing for, and cost recovery of, water supply and sanitation infrastructure."32 Scholars recognize; "Highly corrupt countries tend to under-invest in human capital by spending less on education, over-investing in public infrastructure relative to private investment, and degrading environmental quality."33

Thirsty For Change:

Mexico's new President Andrés Manuel López Obrador is well aware corruption heavily burdens his people and their national economy, declaring; *"corruption is the most important thing because it's eating away at the country in every way imaginable."*[34] Obrador appears to agree with another observer who writes: "The common Mexican phrase "El que no tranza no avanza," or *"The one that does not cheat, does not succeed,"* must be extinguished from Mexican society."[35] Perhaps Mexican President Lopez-Obrador's NaturAMLO initiative is evidence of his public recognition of the devastating influence of corruption on Mexico's natural resources and their impacts on public health?

The Lopez-Obrador NaturAMLO declaration in 2018 is not the first of its kind Mexico. Unfortunately, it is another in a long history of kind Mexican governmental proclamations to clean up the environment. In 1988, Mexico formally instituted their Ecology Law as a tangible display of the national commitment to "confront the problems of the deteriorating quality of the natural environment."[36] In 1988, the author prognosticated; "even basic local services, such as drinking water, garbage collection and disposal, and sewage treatment, will continue to be deficient and deteriorate further; official efforts to reduce air and water pollution are just beginning and still quite inadequate."[37]

Unfortunately, now three decades later, although progress has been made by Mexico, the results remain unsatisfactory. Degradation of natural resources continues. Ecosystem deterioration continues unabated. In 2017, the OECD observes: "Substantial investment will be needed to provide and sustain water security and safeguard economic activities, urban centres, and freshwater ecosystems that depend on water resources."[38]

Mexico is thirsty for tangible change.

The Toilet Assumption

As it relates to corruption and the environmental and tangible public health hazards that emanate therefrom, Mexico is not unlike many other countries. It remains enmeshed in the miasma of what sociologist Philip Slater has termed the toilet assumption: *"the notion that unwanted matter, unwanted difficulties, unwanted complexities and obstacles will disappear if they're removed from our immediate field of vision."*[39] It is the result of a history of deeply embedded, systemic enmeshment of misguided belief and unproductive practice; "once flushed out of sight, (these problems) cease to exist."40 Unfortunately, water is biologically essential for human existence. When the source, availability, quality, distribution and stewardship of water become degraded, a process has begun. Unless interrupted by human intervention, the degradation process will continue. This leads to incalculable costs to human health, economic viability, and political stability. Throughout the degradation process, unforeseen costs continue to accumulate. As an outcome of public corruption, the costs associated with ignoring, granting lip service to, managing appearances, or deferring effective water resource stewardship - can be flushed out of sight. However obscure their existence may have been treated in the past, they exist. They are cumulative. Until, one day, a country officially awakens and realizes that flushing the costs simply doesn't work anymore. The plumbing for a society's ability to flush the reality is plugged. The overflow from the practice of flushing now accumulates where we stand. It's unmistakable. People are getting sick. People are dying. The future is at risk. The cost of forestalling the required solutions is unbearable. It is the moment a country recognizes and implements the required comprehensive remedies...or continues to attempt to flush what cannot be flushed any longer.

In Mexico today, President Lopez-Obrador has taken a stand that led to his election. He is unwilling to accept the multi-dimensional practices of corruption in his country. The hopes of the Mexican people float on the prospects for the reduction of corruption, as well as the funding required to implement his **NatuAMLO** environmental restoration initiative.41

The term "**C**lean **U**p **T**he **E**nvironment" (hereinafter "CUTE") has become a phrase used by politicians globally to denote a concern that may play well at the polls, but rarely turns into measurable improvements for endangered and polluted ecosystems. Frankly, Lake Chapala is a national treasure of Mexico. It is a global treasure. It is an area inhabited by people from all around the globe. The health and welfare of millions are dependent upon the restoration of these waters and this basin.42 The conundrum legitimately demands a cure versus any more cute treatment;
Chapala **U**rgently **R**equires the **E**xtraordinary: a national political directive that moves from the lip-service of cute, to the demonstrable remediation and enduring pride delivered by the CURE. The administration of

Mexico's President Andrés Manuel López Obrador (AMLO) has the opportunity to declare that Lake Chapala deserves the designation as a site for the CURE: **C**omprehend the **U**rgency to **R**estore the **E**cosystem. Perhaps the Lake Chapala basin will be the first tangible step in the roll-out of AMLO's NaturAMLO promise to the people of Mexico. However, as one author observes in another context: Mexico "should first accept that the path followed has been wrong. Mexico cannot solve its problems with the same theory that provoked them."43

Thus, the human ability for *thinking* about resident environmental and public health hazards in Mexico related to water (and corruption) must be re-examined. Some scholars suggest; "a growing chorus calls for a fundamental reassessment of how we should understand and combat corruption, often framed in terms of the need to "rethink" existing approaches."44 Unfortunately, in Mexico, as in many developing countries, economic development is prioritized over natural resource protection – and rehabilitation. However, water is not discretionary for human life. Yet, its' preservation and restoration is treated as discretionary spending. As outcomes of corruption, the correlation becomes even more muddled. Why?

Corruption Cognition – A Rethinking:

The facts are clear; the outcomes of the public health and environmental hazards resident in Lake Chapala are the result of a long series of human choices, human decisions. How we humans *think* about corruption and its relationship to a myriad of impacts on, and overexploitation of, natural resources, requires *rethinking*.45 One observer notes: "anticorruption efforts represent a huge policy failure: there seems little evidence that we are much closer to resolving the issue in 2017 than we were in 1996."46 Thu s, if our actions are ineffective, it may be wise to re-examine that which precedes our actions.

In regard to our human capacities to think, the term cognition is defined as: "a term referring to the mental processes involved in gaining knowledge and comprehension. These processes include thinking, knowing, remembering, judging and problem-solving. These are higher-level functions of the brain and encompass language, imagination, perception, and planning."47 The point is, how we think about the realities of social problems in life, is fundamental in determining how we speak about them, and inquire about their form, presence and management. Our thinking about social problems comes alive in our conversations, narratives, studies of the problem, and the recommendations we make regarding public policy intended to prevent, manage, reduce or eradicate these problems. Thinking (a silent, non-verbal mental activity) becomes audible and visible in human life. It then becomes the basis for our actions. Our actions – and our inactions - reflect our thinking. What we think inhabits the stories we share with one another amidst the maze of social contexts within which we humans interact.

Humans have been referred to as the great ape with a mind designed for story- telling. We have been characterized by the term Homo Fictus or fiction man; or *The Story Telling Animal*."[48] To possess the ability to tell stories, you must have a biological capacity to think, wonder, ponder, to question, to have the desire and ability to express yourself. According to those much brighter than me, "it all began about 70,000 years ago, when the Cognitive Revolution enabled Sapiens to start talking about things that existed only in their imagination."[49]

Oftentimes, words serve to change the tenor of both our thinking and our dialog. Sometimes they change the way we perceive world, self and others. The best one's change our behavior for the better. We overlook the fact that humans create language – and that the process of creating language is ongoing. It's our privilege and responsibility. Enter "Knowmentary."[50] If the history of human civilization demonstrates anything – in any knowledge discipline - it is the fact that what we think we know is momentary. It's temporary. It is *knowmentary*. Knowledge, beliefs, values, attitudes, perceptions, observations, practices, policies, mores, memes and norms are all perishable. Even emotions appear and disappear in terms of their actual behavioral expressions by humans. The degree to which we think we know: terms like certain, truth, love, affection, rejection, doubt, fear and confusion also ebb and flow as emotional states expressed in human existence. Knowmentary is applicable to the current state of the study of corruption, its origins, forms, impacts, costs, prevention, reduction and management in societies.

As an example of the application of knowmentary to the study of the social phenomenon of corruption; "**Rational choice theory** has long dominated the academic study of corruption, anti-corruption practice and policy approaches. It explains corruption as the function of calculating, strategic, self-interested behaviour."51 However, the overwhelming weight of the available evidence (particularly from the field of behavioral economics and applied psychology) has debunked the myth of humans as rational actors who choose rational choices. Thus, if we conclude that the basis for our assumptions about human behavior that underlie our approach to understanding corruption is flawed, we require a reorientation in our thinking. As one author says; "when people believe a conclusion is true, we are also very likely to believe arguments that appear to support it, even when these arguments are unsound."52

Thus, if our assumptions about "human nature are the problem," perhaps reorienting our view of "human nature is also the solution."53 Corruption is just one form of deception. Deception involves lying. As one expert declares; "Everyone lies. Everyone. Almost every form of life on Earth has a means of camouflaging itself, most often for self-preservation. The chameleon. The worm. The house cat. The grasshopper. Even plants lie, for goodness sake."54 Yes, even governments lie. Governments are groups of humans charged with making decisions for the benefit of their constituencies. Deception is deeply ingrained our species. Governments are no exception; "We are more capable than any other species of self-deception and illusion, of fooling ourselves even while we are trying to avoid being fooled by nature."55 Mexico is simply another nation, among multitudes, where expressions of deception as a fundamental component of pervasive corruption, resides. What are some of the lies we tell ourselves regarding environmental and public health hazards as outcomes of corruption? Here are a few:

- Nothing can be done. We're powerless.
- We must accept and tolerate these outcomes.
- It's not my problem.
- It's just the part of the price of progress.
- It can wait.
- Water is everywhere. Don't worry about it.
- This is simply another longstanding, divisive issue in our society.

In confronting the elements of deception above, we must identify the elements of the essential narrative to counteract it. These elements include:

- *We* can do this – *together*. Here's the list of what must be done now.56
- The reality is unacceptable and intolerable.
- It's our problem. I am getting involved.
- Progress now requires immediate, renewed, comprehensive intervention.
- People are getting sick. People are dying. Waiting is over. Half-baked, ineffective measures won't cut it anymore. Water quality and supply is essential for the future stability and economic vitality of Mexico as a nation. It is both a patriotic and moral duty to intervene.
- The condition of the water in the lake Chapala basin will continue to degrade without immediate, sustained, human intervention. It is critically imperiled and may be lost as a strategically essential asset for Mexico.
- The rehabilitation and restoration opportunity in the Lake Chapala basin will act as a cohesive, uniting inspiration for the Mexican federal government, and its people.

Yet, let's remember: "the human capacity for deceit and self-deception are universal. No human group has a monopoly on the disease, nor is anyone immune."57 The myths, assumptions and lies that inhabit our thinking about environmental and public health hazards as outcomes of corruption come alive in the policy considerations we advance to address the same. Yet, the result is toxic, as this author points out; "The lie is attempted again. And again it succeeds. And so begins a very slippery transition from harmless lying into the smooth ease of toxic deception."58

Embracing knowmentary in our pursuit of a better understanding of corruption provides us with the essential permission to press on beyond the boundaries of what we think we currently know. It encourages us to critically examine our current assumptions, attitudes, practices, approaches and beliefs. It provides the courage to confront and dispose of our historical affection for the toilet assumption. It is a tool that allows us to discard the non-essential baggage of carrying on with the disposable weight of what we think we know, allowing us the essential mobility to explore the yet to be discovered beyond the current horizons of our understanding. Knowmentary allows us to be forgiven for treading water in the safe harbors of our past certainties, and allows us to confess our appreciation for what we have yet to comprehend beyond the breakwater. Knowmentary is non-judgmental; it is not concerned with the distribution of shame or blame. It is inclusive and inviting, celebrating the prospects for new, refreshing, multi-disciplinary collaborations directed toward the subject of corruption in society.

Environmental and Public Health Hazards as Consequences of Corruption:

In Mexico, (as in many other developing nations) environmental degradation and the documented public health hazards associated therewith are consequences of corruption. In this respect, they are outcomes representing the tension in balancing limited national economic resources, economic growth, preserving and protecting natural resources, and the maintenance of political power. When we arrive at a critical juncture where a country must address the rehabilitation and restoration of strategically imperative sources of drinking water – well – nobody ever imagined what those costs might entail.59

Fortunately, our insights into actual corruption in Mexico are not limited to simply national scandal and cartel activity. Researchers in the physical sciences have labored for decades in the Lake Chapala basin documenting pollution, invasive species, and presence of heavy metals, pesticides, agrichemicals, species contamination, and coliform content in these waters. Public health scientific endeavors have laid bare the epidemic of Chronic Kidney Disease and other diseases that users of these waters contract. NGO's and non-profits work diligently with impacted communities. However, even with a robust body of evidence from both the physical and social sciences, those dedicated to human services, international organizations, and a myriad of advocacy groups - the essential national recognition of the necessity to address the urgency of the Lake Chapala basin restoration challenge remains absent. Why?

A quote from the Water Integrity Network captures the essence of the current challenge in Mexico:

> "A dysfunctional state apparatus – *lack of supervision, incompetence and corruption in the public sector – affects the water supply and sanitation sector in most parts of the world. It impacts all aspects of the sector, from a household's access opportunities and the state's provision of water for domestic*

use, to infrastructure for water treatment, and distribution and resource management. It is estimated that corrupt and dishonest practices globally deplete the water sector by "as much as 30–40 percent in 'highly corrupt' countries"60

In Mexico (and other nations), the human right to clean drinking water has been treated as discretionary spending. Withholding the essential expenditures in this arena, including preserving and protecting the current supply, its distribution, and insuring that discharges of pollutants are effectively regulated has been ineffective. As another author points out, the absence of the essential delivery of country resources is, in fact, a form of corruption, and a violation of the United Nations resolution declaring safe drinking water and sanitation are a legal Human Right; "Insufficient expenditure or misallocation of public resources which results in the non-enjoyment of the right to water by individuals or groups, particularly the vulnerable or marginalized."61 Mexico certainly has an established apparatus to do so. However, the results produced by state, federal and municipal regulatory officials are abysmal, as evidenced by the cesspool that Lake Chapala has unfortunately become. Mexico's governmental entities have benefited from this mismanagement and misallocation of financial resources and have managed an appearance of attempting to deliver on their charter. They have failed. Their collective failures can be aptly described as public corruption, whereby; "corruption occurs when an official charged with a public responsibility operates in his or her own interest in a way that undermines the program's aims."62 This form of corruption causes the outcomes of environmental and public health hazards that inhabit the Lake Chapala basin. The goals and objectives of the myriad of water policy regulators, programs and objectives have been compromised, as evidenced by the absence of tangible, positive results. As one scholar notes; "corruption comprises the mechanisms that undermine the goals of public programs, whatever those goals may be."63 Water quality and waste water/sewage treatment are big business in Mexico, as represented by the budget of CONAGUA, referenced at the beginning of this article. Yet, "Large agencies and the agencies responsible for regulating the construction sector are found to be most vulnerable to corruption."64

In Mexico today, President Lopez-Obrador has the opportunity to redefine the reality outlined below:

"Corruption is a symptom of a larger disease — the failure of institutions and governance, resulting in poor management of revenues and resources and an absence of delivery of public goods and services. We must think beyond anti-corruption rhetoric and traditional tactics. We need to be more strategic and rigorous, identifying and addressing corruption's underlying causes and examining the weaknesses in key institutions and government policies and practices. We have to focus our efforts on the broader context of governance and accountability. Only then can we see the many other shapes and forms corruption can take and address this epidemic."[65]

How?

Corralling Corruption

According to The Baker Institute-Mexico Center scholar Dr. Jose Ivan Rodriguez-Sanchez:[66]

"*In order to combat corruption, prevent it from being systematized, and diminish its negative impact on Mexico's development, it is important to develop effective public policies. Punishing corruption is also a key element of any effective anticorruption policy. The public and private sectors need to increase the probability of being caught, as well as the penalties for corrupt acts. In addition, incentives must be provided to insiders that report corrupt acts, and their protection must be ensured.*"[67]

The policy considerations for corralling corruption are widely available and abundant. I will leave that subject area for others to address. The literature on the prevention, detection and prosecution of corrupt acts in society related to natural resources is abundant. However, the literature on the urgency for rethinking the restoration and rehabilitation of Mexico's strategic water resources is substantially less apparent. Yet, Mexico is not alone in this sense. A cross-cultural look at another example of mismanagement of water resources that produce public health hazards is appropriate here.

Accountability – The Flint, Michigan USA Approach

In the recent/ongoing Flint, Michigan USA water fiasco, Special prosecutor Todd Flood declared: *"There was a clear, willful and wanton disregard... knowing that someone was going to get sick, someone was going to die."* And they sat on the information, and that being specifically Director Nick Lyon."68 Lyons, among other public officials, are now criminally charged, including involuntary manslaughter, for their roles and mishandling of one of the worst environmental and public health crises related to water.69

Involuntary Manslaughter is defined as: *manslaughter resulting from the failure to perform a legal duty expressly required to safeguard human life, from the commission of an unlawful act not constituting a felony, or from the commission of a lawful act in a negligent or improper manner.*70 As indicated by the Flint Michigan public corruption case (and many others), societies are turning to remedies available in the criminal justice process to hold people accountable for their actions, inactions and/or deceptions regarding known public health and environmental hazards. The human costs of these water related crises are difficult to compute yet, they are real and substantial. In pure economic terms, it has been estimated that the economic costs of the Flint water debacle could exceed U.S. $300 billion.71 It is incredibly expensive to ignore and/or mismanage burgeoning public health and environmental hazards; *knowing that someone was going to get sick, someone was going to die...And sitting on the information.*72

Lake Chapala – Jalisco, Mexico

The most glaring example of the Mexican national government's ongoing disregard for known, urgently serious, public health and environmental hazards is centered in the critically important Lerma-Chapala basin in the state of Jalisco. The hazards in this region are multi-dimensional and multi-causal. In this region, people are getting sick, people are dying, and public officials continue to *fail to perform a legal duty expressly required to safeguard human life.*

Examples of the severity of hazardous conditions in this region include the following: Sewage and wastewater plants discharge untreated waste into Lake Chapala; hair samples from indigenous populations around Lake Chapala indicate the presence of unhealthy levels of toxic metals and pesticides; samples of fish and avian species73 contain the same; untreated

Chronic Kidney Disease is endemic74; municipalities do not possess the required financial resources to operate sewage and wastewater treatment plants. The list goes on and on.

According to a recently published in a 2018 report from the Institute of Technology and Higher Studies of the West (ITESO), the following is pertinent:

Lake Chapala does not meet any of the standards that protect the health of both people and ecosystems, in relation to the parameter priority of Fecal Coliforms (COLI_FEC).... in relation to this priority parameter, life is not being protected.75

In Mexico's Lerma-Chapala basin, another form of corruption is resident. As defined in a study by the World Bank, "Corruption jeopardizes the allocation of resources to sectors crucial for development. This diversion of resources typically comes at the expense of the less corruptible social sectors, such as health and education, and thus at the expense of the country's development."76 Such is the reality in this region of Mexico. More specifically, the OECD's guidance is urgent here: "Currently, water policy implementation is uneven. River basin councils are not fully operational twenty years after their creation, the regulatory framework for drinking water and sanitation is scattered across multiple actors, and harmful subsidies in other sectors (energy, agriculture) create a perverse incentive for over-exploitation."77

One observer notes: *"The fight against corruption is a multilateral responsibility, and it needs a new kind of creative and positive leadership from different sectors of society to ensure systemic change."78* This is as true for addressing known public health and environmental hazards, as it is for any other form of corruption where *knowing that someone was going to get sick, someone was going to die...And sitting on the information.79*

When government officials are "disloyal to the public interest or common good,"80 and said disloyalty results in maintaining the ever increasing severity of known public health and environmental hazards...this is a distinct and viral form of corruption. It is also involuntary manslaughter, defined as *resulting from the failure to perform a legal duty expressly required to safeguard human life* by virtue of negligence and/or recklessness on the part of responsible government officials. In terms an element to the solution of "how" in this matter, the legal framework to hold both government agencies, and their primary administrators accountable, is an imperative dimension of redress and re-engineering the approach in Mexico.

Recent developments in China serve as a reference for Mexico. In a 2018 speech, Chinese President Xi Jinping "promised to deploy the full weight of the state to reverse decades of environmental damage, forcing several ministries and regulators to draw up their own plans to fight pollution."81 In the first 10 months of 2018, China has increased its prosecution of persons (8,500) for pollution-related crimes. These prosecutions have also involved financial penalties. According to the Chinese Environment Ministry, these fines total 10.63 billion yuan (US $1.53 billion).

The current reality of the state of environmental degradation and public health hazards in the Lake Chapala basin are outcomes of public corruption - *resulting from the failure to perform a legal duty expressly required to safeguard human life* by virtue of negligence and/or recklessness on the part of responsible government officials. All the evidence is in. Now what?

The Human Right to Water – A Verdict

Within Mexico, efforts are under way to leverage the influence of national and international law to forge essential improvements. The urgency and seriousness of the situation in the Lake Chapala basin recently garnered the attention of the **Latin American Water Council**. During the week of October 22 to 26, 2018, it convened a session of formal Court Hearings of the Latin American Water Court in Guadalajara.

This body found; "The Mexican State, by promoting an urban-industrial and agro-productive extractive model that favors private interest over the public, has led to the deterioration of the quality and quantity of water in rivers, bodies of water and aquifers, with serious impacts on human health, on the production of food and in the conservation of ecosystems. As a consequence, it has unfulfilled with its obligations to respect, guarantee and protect the rights humans to water and sanitation, to health, to food, to housing and environment and, above all, has affected the most vulnerable social groups as are the indigenous and peasant peoples."82

In the recommendations section of this verdict, The Court stated (among others): "That the Mexican State comply with its obligations to respect, protect and guarantee the human rights to water, sanitation, housing, feeding, the environment and the health of the inhabitants of Lake Chapala. That the Mexican State comply with its obligations to respect, protect and guarantee the human rights to water, sanitation, housing, feeding, the environment and the health of the inhabitants of Lake Chapala. That the federal and state health authorities will prepare an epidemiological study that analyzes the specific health damages generated by the use of water and other agents in all the communities surrounding the Lake of Chapala."83

Implementing The Anti-Corruption Framework

In July 2016, Mexican President Enrique Peña Nieto approved the National Anti-Corruption System (Sistema Nacional Anticorrupción, SNA), the country's anti-corruption enforcement machinery. It has yet to be fully implemented as of December 2018. The purpose of the SNA is to "coordinate and enforce anti-corruption efforts in all levels of government—municipal, state, and federal."84 This implementation requires a transition from Mexico's federal Attorney General's Office (Procuraduría General de la República, PGR) to a new, independent National Prosecutor's Office (Fiscalía General de la República). This new office will be separate from the executive branch, enhancing impartiality in investigations and prosecutions of corruption. Currently, there are numerous vacancies in the adequate staffing of this new unit.85

Implementing anti-corruption mechanisms at the federal level of governance in Mexico is certainly an improvement. However, other levels of government remain concerns, as evidenced by comments from the President of the Mexican Employers' Federation, Gustavo de Hoyos. He observes that most states in Mexico have made "little progress" regarding the implementation of the strategy. He adds; "A substantial part of fighting corruption is within the scope of states and municipalities, where there are large discretionary margins in the management of public resources because of a lack of checks, balances and accountability."86

Conclusions

The ongoing denial of the essential array of resources the Lerma-Chapala basin so desperately requires in Mexico, is unconscionable. However, the hopes of the Mexican people have soared, supporting the election of President Lopez-Obrador. May President Andrés Manuel López Obrador recognize and act upon the cumulative effects of the absence of action by his predecessors, and declare and oversee the rehabilitative strategies that this region in Mexico so desperately deserves.

The presence, degree of severity, and absence of legitimate government interventions regarding known public health and environmental hazards in Mexico are, in fact, products of public corruption. As one expert notes; "Mexicans must also continue to pressure their government to identify and punish corrupt acts."87 The development of a National Development Plan by April 2019 – will embody that National Infrastructure Plan that will define the Mexico's water resource management strategy.88 Perhaps the framework and essence of this article will motivate leaders like President Lopez-Obrador to re-examine how the absence of the essential allocation of government resources unequivocally leads to the unabated increasing severity of existing public health and environmental hazards that harm their people, their nation, and their future. I hope so.

As the OECD documents: "Inadequate water supply and sanitation, together with a rise in pollution, increase mortality and morbidity, raise water treatment costs, lower productivity and inhibit freshwater ecosystems' capacity to deliver valuable ecosystem services (including their ability to process pollutants)."89

The ongoing contribution of journalists is imperative in challenging various dimensions of corruption in Mexico. Journalists provide voice to voiceless compromised bodies of water, ecosystems, species, habitats and the people they support. The pervasive sense of powerlessness that corruption engenders over the necessity and possibility for rehabilitation and restoration of these areas is revealed for what it is by journalists; a veil that can be lifted revealing realistic hope worthy of advocacy that positively raises awareness and results in inspiration for action.

Yet, a note of caution: "We need to stop searching for unicorns. By this, I mean any attempt to identify "the answer" to how we should combat corruption, exemplified by the various lists. There is now a consensus that one-size-fits-all approaches are doomed to failure, and yet the temptation to develop prescriptive approaches remains deeply embedded, and anticorruption "toolkits" abound." 90

The reality of the current environmental and public health hazards that ravage this area represent the tangible opportunity to prioritize restoration and rehabilitation of this habitat as a very public and legitimate form of the Mexican governments' fight against corruption by dealing with this present day outcome of corruption. This approach evidences the essential rethinking that the outcomes of corruption represent. Particularly when embodied in compromised, essential water resources of strategic national importance, and the documented public health hazards associated therewith, which require immediate and comprehensive Mexican federal government directed interventions.

Translation: Fix the outcome before it cannot be fixed. Shift the focus downstream. Work upstream from there. Provide the essential medical treatment the victims require. Educate the public about the current hazards associated with drinking, cooking and bathing in this water. Require consumer warnings on fish harvested from the lake and food products irrigated with this water. Stop the application of pesticides on the invasive species that choke the lake.91 Supply the essential non-chemical equipment required to harvest and safely dispose of invasive plant species removed from the lake. Provide alternative sources of water for indigenous communities who represent the most vulnerable. Upgrade waste water and sewage treatment plants around the lake. Insure their proper functioning, operation and management. Provide federal funding and oversight for their operations. Reimagine clean water distribution, sewage and waste water treatment for the communities that surround the lake. Insure that any future development in the region does not increase the stress on the currently overburdened infrastructure.

Immediate intervention in Mexico's Lake Chapala region is required. Of course, as the corruption literature indicates, Mexico needs to vastly improve governance enhancements based upon transparency, accountability and integrity. The situation demands a wholesale reorganization of the current bureaucracy chartered with the management, preservation and restoration of Mexico's strategically imperative water resources. It requires uncommon courage and a rethinking. It requires a national leader to take a stand. It may start in Mexico with a new President

- and his new understanding of the urgency in intervening, arresting with conviction, the ongoing environmental degradation and the life threatening public health hazards associated therewith in the Lerma-Chapala basin.

People are getting sick. People are dying. Such is the reality of environmental and public health hazards as outcomes of corruption.

Imagine

As Mexico moves forward in addressing this malady, it is imperative that we imagine the possibilities the positive outcomes hold. As one author notes; "we need to change the terms of the conversation and accentuate the positive, rather than only trying to eliminate the negative."[92] We must rethink the current precariously fragile state of the waters in the Lake Chapala basin. As legitimate outcomes of corruption in Mexico, these environmental and public health hazards must be addressed where they reside; downstream from the complexities of the sources of corruption. We must begin the immediate and comprehensive remediation and restoration efforts here. We then work upstream. The total destruction of this vitally strategic natural resource for Mexico can and must be stopped. If this resource is destroyed, it will not be due to a failure of the human imagination; it will be a failure of the human will.

Imagine Lake Chapala restored to a healthy body of clean water. Imagine children safely swimming in the water. Imagine the eradication of Chronic Kidney Disease. Imagine the joy and pride of millions of Mexicans that the primary source of water for the Guadalajara metropolitan area has been restored. Imagine...

EPILOGUE

"In a world where the forces that seek to divide us are strong, I came to one conclusion: We have to save each other. It's the only way to save ourselves."1

I'd like to conclude this work reiterating what I stated at the outset:

"It should be stated from the outset that I adore Mexico; particularly - Guadalajara in the State of Jalisco. The people, culture, food, art, architecture and landscapes are precious to me. I did not travel to Mexico with this book in mind. The inspirations for this book found me – my heart and my mind. The motivation for this book was both unexpected and unintentional. Yet, when confronted with these realities, I knew I must write about them. Mexico is not unlike any other country on the planet; it possesses extraordinary positives it is proud to share with the world – and – it has current issues that it would rather not speak about. I encountered both."

There's hardly a place remaining on this planet that is not infected by severe environmental or public health hazards. Yet, when considering a place to retire, I decided to invest the time, resources and energy required to look beneath the surface of the Lake Chapala area. This was our first choice. It's not anymore.

My wife says I walk around with a *"crap detector"* swiveling atop my head in a 360 on a 24/7 basis. That doesn't mean I'm a cynic. I'm not. It does mean that during my undergraduate and graduate studies I was trained to think critically. What that doesn't mean is to look for evil lurking around every corner, be untrusting, or think negatively. What it does mean is to use the intellectual and emotional faculties you have been gifted with to evaluate the choices you encounter in life...particularly when that choice involves moving to another country for the rest of your days with your most precious gift in life. For me, that's my wife - and our two Labrador Retrievers.

What I encountered in the Lake Chapala area were some of the nicest folks you might ever want to meet. The thing that got my attention is that those involved in selling real estate to couples like us, or other local folks who had a vested interest in promoting the area – never had a weakness, inconvenience or critical thing to share with us. We heard stuff like "paradise, eternal spring, best climate on the planet, lots of folks just like you, the airport is close," and the like. That caused my crap detector to activate. So, I decided I had to dig beneath the surface of those representations. This book is the result of that endeavor.

As I wrote about my findings, and shared the same with others, I began to receive email from folks. The vast majority of this correspondence expressed sincere gratitude – and encouraged me to look at other aspects of the issues I had written about.

Every destination has its strengths and weaknesses. The reality of *Lake Chapala – Beneath The Surface* - is no different. As I stated in the Prologue to this book, the social media resources typically referenced by prospective North American retirees are, in my opinion, inherently biased – emphasizing the positives. The other thing about social media resources for those considering retirement in Mexico is that they are dated/not current. When they are current, it's typically another positive spin article designed to attract you versus share some objective strengths and weaknesses with you. When considering retirement to another country, it's important to seek an objective view of the current reality. That takes a *ton* of time and effort. We invested just that in what has turned out to be the book you are reading. My hope is that it further informs your due diligence. A good book prompts dialog and additional questions to pursue. I hope this book does that for you. Finally, know this; Mexico can.

Please know that wherever you might relocate to for your retirement, our hope for you and yours is more joy, good health, laughter, smiles, great meals, amazing vistas, and safe travels.

May you also attempt to make a positive contribution to the lives of other folks.

My wife says that's why I had to write this book.

Be well.

Bill Dahl – January 2019

A CAUTIONARY NOTE

Writing about issues some people would prefer to remain beneath the surface can be a risky endeavor. This is particularly true in Mexico (and other countries). According to numerous sources, "Mexico remains among the world's most dangerous places for journalists."[2] The environment for media in Mexico is not considered free (by numerous international sources). For journalists, Mexico has one of the highest murder rates on the planet. It is ranked as one of the top 10 deadliest countries worldwide for people who work in the media.[3] According to Reporters Without Borders, Mexico has a worse ranking for journalist safety than either Afghanistan or South Sudan.[4]

While on-site in Mexico, I did not disclose my journalist credentials or identify myself as such. I did carry around my Canon DSLR wherever I went (I advise against this). Upon my return to the U.S., I did disclose my role as an investigative journalist. In some cases, upon request, I provided documentation to sources to validate the same. I had requests NOT to mention certain names of persons who provided assistance to me in this endeavor…both Mexican nationals and persons from other countries.

You have likely heard it said that "everyone has a phone today so everybody is a photographer," or "everyone has a keyboard today so everyone is a journalist." Of course, neither of these statements is accurate. However, when out in public places in Mexico, with a phone or camera, you may inadvertently capture a photograph of someone who desires not to be photographed. (Granted, for authentic photographers and photojournalists, I always ask permission first, from an adult, particularly if it is a child I am requesting permission to photograph). People who have inadvertently captured photos of persons in Mexico who do not desire the same have become unwitting victims of retaliatory acts. Be careful.

Please be cautious about free speech in Mexico, especially if your expressions are in writing, published in the media, or via social media platforms.

FINAL THANKS

No book is the product of one mind, sitting in a room picking away at a keyboard. This book is no exception.

Special thanks to Gabriel Vazquez-Sanchez of AIPROMADES in Guadalajara. Enrique Lira Coronado - Coordinador de Enlace Institucional y Comunitario y Servidor de los Pueblos Foro Socioambiental GDL deserves thanks as well.. Both read drafts of the chapters contained herein and added valuable insights, additional materials to refer to, and edits. To the dozens upon dozens of people (who shall remain unnamed), whom I interviewed, sent emails, posted encouragement (and criticisms) on social media sites as I mused through this mass of material – Muchos Gracias.

To *Reggie*, my 11 year old Black Lab, and *Reno,* our 16 month old, 136 lb. Pyrador (Pure Bred Great White Pyrenees =Father and Pure Bred Chocolate Lab = Mother). Both were graciously my constant, bored, companions as their dad sat typing on his laptop for a few months...at all hours. I will make it up to them!

To Dr. Jose Ivan Rodriguez-Sanchez from Rice University's James A. Baker III Institute for Public Policy – Mexico Center - whose scholarship inspired me to move ahead with this project, and examine my suspicions regarding environmental and public health hazards as legitimate products of the cumulative effects of a myriad of forms of corruption. Dr. Rodriguez-Sanchez also graciously reviewed my chapter entitled: Corruption in Mexico: Environmental and Public Health Hazards As Outcomes of Corruption. He also granted me an extensive interview that adds to both the texture and content of this book. I am deeply grateful Ivan.

Finally, to my wife Jacki: It's no small feat to live with a researcher, investigator, advocate, journalist and writer. If you think a writer's life is an atypical existence, just talk to their spouse!

ABOUT THE AUTHOR

Bill Dahl is married to his BEST friend Jacki. They Live in Central Oregon. They have two Lab retrievers. Bill enjoys reading, research, writing, photography, sports on television, fly-fishing, family, friends, food, laughter and travel.

Bill earned a Bachelor's (Cum Laude) and Master's Degree in Criminal Justice from Washington State University. He was a Research Assistant in the Social Research Center at WSU and a Teaching Assistant. He has taught at the community college and university levels in the U.S. His numerous books, articles and working papers have been published widely. His photography has won so many awards we have lost count. During his business and consulting career he was employed as a lead independent consultant to both privately held and public companies. He was also employed as a Senior Vice President for The Chrysler Corporation and Nations Bank/Bank of America.

The three people I want to have lunch with (at the same time) are John Stewart, Barack Obama, and John Heilemann.

RESEARCH RESOURCES – LAKE CHAPALA

The following is a <u>short</u> list of the studies, reports, articles and working papers that have been completed regarding Lake Chapala – and pertinent to the content of this book. It is *by no means* complete or comprehensive. It does include studies that focus on water quality, the presence of heavy metals, human health, aquatic species, avian species, proposed developments, and invasive plant species. The purpose of this section is to be a guide for you and yours to encourage you to conduct further explorations of the studies and writings that have been completed on these topics. Where I have not provided links, simply use your preferred search engine. Use the endnotes to each chapter for additional resources. Use this book as just one tool in your toolbox. Conduct your own independent research. Come to your own conclusions.

2018-08: Quality Data Analysis Report: Department of Mathematics and Physics. The title of the research endeavor is: **Report of Water Quality Data Analysis of Lake Chapala**. Tlaquepaque, Jalisco: ITESO. It was **published December 2018**. The authors of this study are: Sánchez-Torres, Juan D .; Nuño-Sánchez, Saúl A .; Martinez-Alvarado, Juan C .; Ruiz-Cruz, Riemann Sánchez-Torres, J.D .; Nuño-Sánchez, S.A .; Martínez-Alvarado, J.C. and Ruiz-Cruz.

Palfrey, Dale Hoyt The Guadalajara Reporter December 27, 2018 "**Urbanization Plans Multiply on Lake Chapala's Shoreline**."
http://theguadalajarareporter.net/index.php/news/news/lake-chapala/52863-urbanization-plans-multiply-on-lake-chapala-s-shoreline

Court Hearings of the Latin American Water Court were held during the week of October 22 to 26, 2018, and once the declarations, proofs, communications from the parties, the Jury of the Latin American Water Court issues its decision in the case. In English: SEE: https://www.billdahl.net/articles/lake-chapala-verdict-of-the-court-of-the-latin-american-water-tribunal-october-2018/?fbclid=IwAR3U4YLT-fg1hmasPwiUJtBF8jPQ-LPHpujFWrP9wC7q2hjjVob3gZcDU0M

https://jasn.asnjournals.org/content/18/6/1922 **Survival among Patients with Kidney Failure in Jalisco, Mexico**, Guillermo Garcia-Garcia, Gregorio Briseño-

Rentería, Victor H. Luquín-Arellan, Zhiwei Gao, John Gill and Marcello Tonelli JASN June 2007, 18 (6) 1922-1927; DOI: https://doi.org/10.1681/ASN.2006121388

https://www.ncbi.nlm.nih.gov/pmc/articles/PMC6127446/ – Kidney Int Rep. 2018 Sep; 3(5): 1027–1029. Published online 2018 Jul 27. doi: [10.1016/j.ekir.2018.07.018] The Tragedy of Having ESRD in Mexico Guillermo Garcia-Garcia1,∗ and Jonathan Samuel Chavez-Iñiguez

https://www.who.int/bulletin/volumes/96/6/17-206441/en/ **The global burden of kidney disease and the sustainable development goals**, Valerie A Luyckx, Marcello Tonelli & John W Stanifer.

Asad, Musa & Dinar , Ariel **The Role of Water Policy in Mexico: Sustainability, Equity, and Economic Growth Considerations**, Sustainable Development Working Paper No. 27, September 2006, The World Bank Latin America and the Caribbean Region Environmentally and Socially Sustainable Development Department,

Adler, David **The War for Mexico's Water**, July 2015. Foreign Policy – https://foreignpolicy.com/2015/07/31/the-war-for-privatization-mexicos-water/

Burton, Tony http://www.mexconnect.com/articles/1263-did-you-know-lake-chapala-under-attack-from-water-hyacinth

https://www.ramsar.org/news/mexico-designates-122nd-and-123rd-ramsar-sites

"Contaminación Agrícola y Erosión en la Cuenca del Lago Chapala," 2013 Corazón de la Tierra

https://www.researchgate.net/publication/327167877_Calculating_long-term_changes_in_Lake_Chapala's_area_and_water_volume_using_remote_sensing_and_field_data

https://www.researchgate.net/publication/319692488_Water_Quality_Index_of_Lake_Chapala_in_Mexico_and_its_potential_risk_to_public_health

Prevalence of Albuminuria in Children Living in a Rural Agricultural and Fishing Subsistence Community in Lake Chapala, Mexico. International Journal of Environmental Research and Public Health 14(12):1577 · December 2017 in a Rural Agricultural and Fishing Subsistence

https://mexiconewsdaily.com/news/heavy-metals-blamed-for-kidney-disease/

https://www.reuters.com/article/us-mexico-health-village/murky-business-a-hunt-for-answers-as-children-fall-sick-around-mexico-lake-idUSKBN1DY11E

https://www.washingtonpost.com/world/the_americas/mexicos-president-elect-promises-to-clean-up-the-environment–and-build-a-new-oil-refinery/2018/09/10/f91ac9d6-a336-11e8-a3dd-2a1991f075d5_story.html?noredirect=on&utm_term=.c4b7aa2fc214

Trasande, Leonardo & Cortés, Juanita & Landrigan, Philip & Abercrombie, Mary & F Bopp, Richard & Cifuentes, Enrique. (**2010**). **Methylmercury exposure in a subsistence fishing community in Lake Chapala, Mexico: An ecological approach**. Environmental health : a global access science source. 9. 1. 10.1186/1476-069X-9-1. Environmental Health 9(1):1 · January 2010□
https://www.ncbi.nlm.nih.gov/pubmed/20064246

Torres-Poché, Zaria & A. Mora, Miguel & J. Taylor, Robert & Alvarez-Bernal, Dioselina. (2016). Tracking Metal Pollution in Lake Chapala: **Concentrations in Water, Sediments, and Fish. Bulletin of Environmental Contamination and Toxicology**. 97. 10.1007/s00128-016-1892-6.

Tapia, Omar & López-Caloca, Alejandra. (2018). **Calculating long-term changes in Lake Chapala's area and water volume using remote sensing and field data**. Journal of Applied Remote Sensing. 12. 1. 10.1117/1.JRS.12.042805.
https://www.researchgate.net/publication/327167877_Calculating_long-term_changes_in_Lake_Chapala's_area_and_water_volume_using_remote_sensing_and_field_data

C Hernández-Peña, C & Lares-Villa, Fernando & de los Santos-Villalobos, Sergio & I Estrada-Alvarado, M & C Artiaga Luna, M & Flores-Tavizón, E & Saúl-Solis, S & Domínguez-Acosta, M & Y Soto-Padilla, M & Yadira, Marisela & Padilla, Soto. (2018). REDUCCIÓN DE CROMO HEXAVALENTE Y DEGRADACIÓN DE ROJO DE METILO POR BACTERIAS AISLADAS DE SEDIMENTOS DEL LAGO DE CHAPALA, MÉXICO HEXAVALENT CHROMIUM REDUCTION AND METHYL RED DEGRADATION BY SEDIMENT ISOLATED BACTERIA FROM THE CHAPALA LAKE, MÉXICO.

Luis Trujillo-Cárdenas, Juan & P. Saucedo-Torres, Nereida & Zarate, Pedro & Rios, Nely & Mendizabal, Eduardo & Gomez-Salazar, Sergio. (2010). **Speciation and Sources of Toxic Metals in Sediments of Lake Chapala**, Mexico. Journal of the Mexican Chemical Society. 54. 79-87.https://www.researchgate.net/publication/262649951_Speciation_and_Sources_of_Toxic_Metals_in_Sediments_of_Lake_Chapala_Mexico

González, Deisy & Alvarez-Bernal, Dioselina & Mora, Miguel & René Buelna Osben, Héctor & Ricardo Ruelas-Insunza, Jorge. (2018). Biomonitoreo de metales pesados en plumas de aves acuáticas residentes del Lago de Chapala, México. Revista Internacional de Contaminación Ambiental. 34. 215-224. 10.20937/RICA.2018.34.02.03. https://www.researchgate.net/publication/324904635_Biomonitoreo_de_metales_pesados_en_plumas_de_aves_acuaticas_residentes_del_Lago_de_Chapala_Mexico

Moncayo-Estrada, Rodrigo & Lyons, John & Escalera-Gallardo, Carlos & Lind, Owen. (2012). Long-term change in the biotic integrity of a shallow tropical lake: A decadal analysis of the Lake Chapala fish community. Lake and Reservoir Management - LAKE RESERV MANAG. 28. 92-104. 10.1080/07438141.2012.661029. https://www.researchgate.net/publication/241731633_Long-term_change_in_the_biotic_integrity_of_a_shallow_tropical_lake_A_decadal_analysis_of_the_Lake_Chapala_fish_community

Vallejo-Rodríguez, Ramiro & León-Becerril, E & Díaz-Torres, Jesús & Hernández-Mena, Leonel & Del Real-Olvera, J & Flores-Payán, V & Martínez-Mendoza, Leonardo & Lopez-Lopez, Alberto. (2017). **Water Quality Index of Lake Chapala in Mexico and its potential risk to public health. https://www.researchgate.net/publication/319692488_Water_Quality_Index_of_Lake_Chapala_in_Mexico_and_its_potential_risk_to_public_health**

Bautista-Avalos, Dinora & Cruz-Cárdenas, Gustavo & Moncayo-Estrada, Rodrigo & Teodoro Silva Garcia, Jose & Estrada-Godoy, Francisco. (2014). **Application of the SWAT model to evaluate the diffuse contamination sources at lake Chapala sub-basin, Mexico**. Revista Internacional de Contaminacion Ambiental. 30. 263-274.https://www.researchgate.net/publication/279031642_Application_of_the_SWAT_model_to_evaluate_the_diffuse_contamination_sources_at_lake_Chapala_sub-basin_Mexico

Moya, Carlos. (2018). **PERSISTENT ORGANIC-COMPOUNDS AND GENETIC DAMAGE IN HEPATOCYTES NUCLEUS FROM Pelycanous erythrorhyncus OF CHAPALA LAKE AND SAYULA LAGOON**. mayo. https://www.researchgate.net/publication/322684350_PERSISTENT_ORGANIC-COMPOUNDS_AND_GENETIC_DAMAGE_IN_HEPATOCYTES_NUCLEUS_FROM_Pelycanous_erythrorhyncus_OF_CHAPALA_LAKE_AND_SAYULA_LAGOON

Reynoso Silva, Monica & Arévalo Hernández, Armando & Moya, Carlos & A Hernández, A & F Velasco, A & Á Moya, C. (2014). **Genetic damage in Goodea atripinnis (Goodeidae) and persistent organic-compounds in both Chapala and Sayula Lakes, in Mexico**. Hidrobiologica. 24. 167-1. https://www.researchgate.net/publication/281749060_Genetic_damage_in_Goodea_atripinnis_Goodeidae_and_persistent_organic-compounds_in_both_Chapala_and_Sayula_Lakes_in_Mexico

Reporte de análisis de datos de calidad del agua del Lago de Chapala Sánchez-Torres, Juan D.; Nuño-Sánchez, Saúl A.; Martínez-Alvarado, Juan C.; Ruiz-Cruz, Riemann En Espanol:
https://rei.iteso.mx/bitstream/handle/11117/5614/Calidad%20del%20agua%20del%20Lago%20de%20Chapala.pdf?sequence=4

Anda, J. de, & Shear, H. (2008). **Challenges Facing Municipal Wastewater Treatment in Mexico. Public Works Management & Policy**, 12(4), 590–598. https://doi.org/10.1177/1087724X08317256

Ontiveros, Jorge & Carolina Ruiz-Fernández, Ana & Sanchez-Cabeza, Joan-Albert & Sericano, José & Hascibe Pérez-Bernal, Libia & Páez-Osuna, Federico & B. Dunbar, Robert & Mucciarone, David. (2018). Recent history of persistent organic pollutants (PAHs, PCBs, PBDEs) in sediments from a large tropical lake. Journal of Hazardous Materials. 10.1016/j.jhazmat.2018.11.010. SEE BELOW:

https://www.sciencedirect.com/science/article/pii/S030438941831029X?via%3Dihub

https://www.globalnature.org/35127/Living-Lakes/America/Lake-Chapala/resindex.aspx

https://www.lonelyplanet.com/thorntree/forums/americas-mexico/mexico/lake-chapala-pollution-report

https://mexiconewsdaily.com/news/kidney-failure-cases-probed-in-jalisco/

Corruption in Mexico: SEE: https://www.bakerinstitute.org/experts/jose-ivan-rodriguezsanchez/

INDEX

ENDNOTES

Chapter TWO

---

1 https://www.cbsnews.com/news/more-americans-are-retiring-outside-the-u-s/ - December 27, 2016 -

2 https://money.usnews.com/money/blogs/on-retirement/articles/2017-10-24/8-reasons-mexico-is-americas-favorite-place-to-retire-abroad - October 24, 2017 by Kathleen Peddicord

3 Handy, Charles *The Age of Paradox* Harvard Business School Press © 1994 p. 221

4 https://mexiconewsdaily.com/news/jalisco-earthquakes-felt-in-three-states/

5 http://geo-mexico.com/?p=10612 - "Retirees and "Residential Tourism" - A Case Study of Chapala-Ajijic in Jalisco - January 6, 2014.

6 http://geo-mexico.com/?p=10612 - "Retirees and "Residential Tourism" - A Case Study of Chapala-Ajijic in Jalisco - January 6, 2014.

7https://seniorplanet.org/aging-out-of-place-in-lake-chapala-mexico/ - April 12, 2017 by Erica Manfred.

8 https://www.housingwire.com/blogs/1-rewired/post/46700-lack-of-retirement-savings-haunts-baby-boomers -

9 Pinker, Steven Blank Slate – The Modern Denial of Human Nature, Penguin Books – An Imprint of Penguin Random House LLC New York, NY Copyright (c) 2002 & 2016 by Steven Pinker, p. 224.

Chapter THREE

10 https://www.cbsnews.com/news/more-americans-are-retiring-outside-the-u-s/ - December 27, 2016

11https://money.usnews.com/money/blogs/on-retirement/articles/2017-10-24/8-reasons-mexico-is-americas-favorite-place-to-retire-abroad - October 24, 2017 by Kathleen Peddicord

12 https://www.seniorliving.org/guides/baby-boomers/

13 https://internationalliving.com/the-best-places-to-retire/ Prentice, Glynna - Mexico Editor September 2018 - The World's Best Places to Retire in 2018.

14 Lloyd, Alycynna - *Lack of Retirement Savings Haunts Baby Boomers, REWIRED,* August 31, 2018 - https://www.housingwire.com/blogs/1-rewired/post/46700-lack-of-retirement-savings-haunts-baby-boomers

15 *How Much Does It Cost to Live in Mexico?* - https://internationalliving.com/countries/mexico/cost-of-living-in-mexico/

16 *Mexican Healthcare is Affordable and Excellent* - https://internationalliving.com/countries/mexico/health-care/

17 Abramson, Alexis Ph.D. - *10 Important Baby Boomer Characteristics and Statistics,* July 2018. https://www.alexisabramson.com/baby-boomers-characteristics-statistics/

Chapter FOUR

1 Lewis, Michael - *The Fifth Risk*, W.W. Norton & Company, Inc. New York, NY Copyright (c) 2018 by Michael Lewis p. 219.

2 Lake Chapala Reporter - October 29, 2018: *ITESO - Lake Chapala Contains High Levels of Arsenic and Coliforms.*

3 https://lakechapalareporter.com/chapala-has-not-paid-for-water-sanitation-in-3-years/

4 October 26,2018 - Lake Chapala Reporter

5 Lewis, Michael - *The Fifth Risk*, W.W. Norton & Company, Inc. New York, NY Copyright (c) 2018 by Michael Lewis p. 75.

6 Email November 22, 2018

7 https://www.researchgate.net/publication/327167877_Calculating_long-term_changes_in_Lake_Chapala's_area_and_water_volume_using_remote_sensing_and_field_data

8 https://www.researchgate.net/publication/319692488_Water_Quality_Index_of_Lake_Chapala_in_Mexico_and_its_potential_risk_to_public_health

10 *Prevalence of Albuminuria in Children Living in a Rural Agricultural and Fishing Subsistence Community in Lake Chapala, Mexico.* International Journal of Environmental Research and Public Health 14(12):1577 · December 2017 in a Rural Agricultural and Fishing Subsistence
10 https://mexiconewsdaily.com/news/heavy-metals-blamed-for-kidney-disease/

11 https://www.reuters.com/article/us-mexico-health-village/murky-business-a-hunt-for-answers-as-children-fall-sick-around-mexico-lake-idUSKBN1DY11E

12 Lewis, Michael - *The Fifth Risk*, W.W. Norton & Company, Inc. New York, NY Copyright (c) 2018 by Michael Lewis p. 68.

13 https://www.reuters.com/article/us-mexico-health-village/murky-business-a-hunt-for-answers-as-children-fall-sick-around-mexico-lake-idUSKBN1DY11E

14 https://www.washingtonpost.com/world/the_americas/mexicos-president-elect-promises-to-clean-up-the-environment--and-build-a-new-oil-refinery/2018/09/10/f91ac9d6-a336-11e8-a3dd-2a1991f075d5_story.html?noredirect=on&utm_term=.c4b7aa2fc214

15 Lewis, Michael - *The Fifth Risk*, W.W. Norton & Company, Inc. New York, NY Copyright (c) 2018 by Michael Lewis p. 75.

Chapter FIVE

1 Jared Diamond, is Professor of Geography at the University of California, Los Angeles. He began his scientific career in physiology and expanded into evolutionary biology and biogeography. He has been elected to the National Academy of Sciences, the American Academy of Arts and Sciences, and the American Philosophical Society. Among his many awards are the National Medal of Science, the Tyler Prize for Environmental Achievement, Japan's Cosmo Prize, a MacArthur Foundation Fellowship, and the Lewis Thomas Prize Honoring the Scientist as Poet, presented by Rockefeller University. He has published more than six hundred articles and his book, **Guns, Germs, and Steel**, was awarded the Pulitzer Prize. This biographical excerpt of Jared Diamond is from: http://www.jareddiamond.org/Jared_Diamond/Welcome.html

2 Diamond, Jared *Collapse – How Societies Choose to Fail or Succeed*, Penguin Books - Published by The Penguin Group New York, NY Copyright © 2005, 2011 by Jared Diamond, p. 425.

3 Diamond, Jared *The Third Chimpanzee – The Evolution and Future of the Human Animal,* Harper Perrenial New York, NY Copyright © 1992 by Jared Diamond, p. 337.

4 Asad, Musa & Dinar , Ariel *The Role of Water Policy in Mexico: Sustainability, Equity, and Economic Growth Considerations*, Sustainable Development Working Paper No. 27, September 2006, The World Bank Latin America and the Caribbean Region Environmentally and Socially Sustainable Development Department, p. 5.

5 Ibid: p. 5.

6 Adler, David *The War for Mexico's Water*, July 2015. Foreign Policy - https://foreignpolicy.com/2015/07/31/the-war-for-privatization-mexicos-water/

7 Diamond, Jared *Collapse – How Societies Choose to Fail or Succeed*, Penguin Books - Published by The Penguin Group New York, NY Copyright © 2005, 2011 by Jared Diamond, p. 438.

8 AIPROMADES - See http://www.Aipromades.org/about - It is the Intermunicipal Association for the Protection of the Environment and Sustainable Development of Lake Chapala

9 Burton, Tony http://www.mexconnect.com/articles/1263-did-you-know-lake-chapala-under-attack-from-water-hyacinth

10 https://www.ramsar.org/news/mexico-designates-122nd-and-123rd-ramsar-sites

11 "Contaminación Agrícola y Erosión en la Cuenca del Lago Chapala," 2013 Corazón de la Tierra.

12 *Steven Pinker* is a Johnstone Family Professor in the Department of Psychology at Harvard University. Pinker is an experimental psychologist who conducts research in visual cognition, psycholinguistics, and social relations. He conducts research on language and cognition, writes for publications such as the *New York Times*, *Time* and *The Atlantic*, and is the author of ten books. Excerpt from: https://stevenpinker.com/biocv

13 Pinker, Steven *The Stuff of Thought - Language As A Window Into Human Culture*, Penguin Books Published by The Penguin Group, New York, NY Copyright (c) 2007 by Steven Pinker p. 4.

14 Ibid p. 4.

Chapter SIX

1 http://www.itesm.mx/wps/wcm/connect/sim/Guadalajara+EN

2 https://jasn.asnjournals.org/content/18/6/1922 Survival among Patients with Kidney Failure in Jalisco, Mexico, Guillermo Garcia-Garcia, Gregorio Briseño-Rentería, Victor H. Luquín-Arellan, Zhiwei Gao, John Gill and Marcello Tonelli JASN June 2007, 18 (6) 1922-1927; DOI: https://doi.org/10.1681/ASN.2006121388

3 https://www.ncbi.nlm.nih.gov/pmc/articles/PMC6127446/ - Kidney Int Rep. 2018 Sep; 3(5): 1027–1029. Published online 2018 Jul

27. doi: [10.1016/j.ekir.2018.07.018] The Tragedy of Having ESRD in Mexico Guillermo Garcia-Garcia1,∗ and Jonathan Samuel Chavez-Iñiguez1

4 https://www.who.int/bulletin/volumes/96/6/17-206441/en/ *The global burden of kidney disease and the sustainable development goals,* Valerie A Luyckx, Marcello Tonelli & John W Stanifer

5 https://translate.google.com/translate?hl=en&sl=es&u=http://wradio.com.mx/emisora/2018/08/24/guadalajara/1535133019_890151.html&prev=search Soriano, Giselle

Chapter SEVEN

1 https://www.google.com/search?q=What+is+a+Boomerang%3F&rlz=1C1JZAP_enUS812US812&oq=What+is+a+Boomerang%3F&aqs=chrome..69i57j0l5.20862j0j7&sourceid=chrome&ie=UTF-8

2 Garcia, Gabriel *That $30 trillion 'great wealth transfer' is a myth, Gabriel Garcia is managing director and head of relationship management at BNY Mellon's Pershing Advisor Solutions , May 22, 2018.* https://www.cnbc.com/2018/05/22/that-30-trillion-great-wealth-transfer-is-a-myth.html

3 PEW Research Center March 1, 2018 The Generation Gap in American Politics, http://www.people-press.org/2018/03/01/the-generation-gap-in-american-politics/

4 Arigoni, Danielle AARP *"Baby boomers are struggling to downsize and it could create the next housing crisis,* https://www.bankrate.com/mortgages/baby-boomer-downsizing-housing-crisis/

5 Friedberg, Barbara A. *Are We in a Baby Boomer Retirement Crisis?* October 21, 2018 Investopedia: https://www.investopedia.com/articles/personal-finance/032216/are-we-baby-boomer-retirement-crisis.asp

6 Mandel, Benjamin & Wu, Livia *The Long and Short of Baby Boomer Balance Sheets –* J.P. Morgan Asset Management, October 2015: The estimates here range from $4.6 to $7 trillion, https://am.jpmorgan.com/gi/getdoc/1383246462222 Garcia (above) debunks the $30 trillion figure.

7 Ibid, Mandel & Wu

8 Kaul, Karan and Goodman, Laurie *Senior Access to Home Equity - February 2017 -* The Urban Institute, p. 2.

https://www.urban.org/sites/default/files/publication/88556/seniors_access_to_home_equity.pdf

9 Lewis, Michael - *The Fifth Risk*, W.W. Norton & Company, Inc. New York, NY Copyright (c) 2018 by Michael Lewis p. 219.

10 National Travel & Tourism Office: https://travel.trade.gov/outreachpages/outbound.general_information.outbound_overview.asp

11 *7 of the Top Places U.S. Expats Are Living in Latin America (and Why)* https://vivatropical.com/nicaragua/where-expats-live-in-central-america/

12 *MSLGroup for The Mexican Tourism Board,*https://www.journeymexico.com/blog/mexico-tourism-facts-statistics-2016

13 https://tradingeconomics.com/mexico/tourism-revenues

14 *Tourism Seen Jumping to No. 3 Mexico Cash Source by 2018:* Bloomberg: https://www.bloomberg.com/news/articles/2013-06-25/tourism-seen-jumping-to-mexico-s-3rd-biggest-cash-source-by-2018

15 https://www.scholastic.com/teachers/articles/teaching-content/mexico-economy/

16 Villarreal, M. Angeles *U.S.-Mexico Economic Relations: Trends, Issues, and Implications* – March 27, 2018 Congressional Research Service, https://fas.org/sgp/crs/row/RL32934.pdf

17 https://www.washingtonpost.com/news/politics/wp/2018/01/12/millions-of-americans-have-moved-overseas-and-its-not-because-the-u-s-is-a-shithole/?utm_term=.cd9bbd1d159b

18 The Business Year - *Over 6,000 Companies in Jalisco – An Interview with Aristóteles Sandoval Díaz* – Who has governed the western State of Jalisco since 2013. Mexico 2018 | ECONOMY | https://www.thebusinessyear.com/mexico-2018/aristoteles-sandoval-diaz-governor-jalisco/vip-interview

19 Aristóteles Sandoval Díaz *Millions of Americans live in Mexico. Can we continue to coexist?* The Guardian January 23, 2017. https://www.theguardian.com/commentisfree/2017/jan/23/trump-futures-mexico-us-interlocked-wall-border

20 *Where Do Mexico's 1 Million U.S. Expats Live?*

https://vivatropical.com/mexico/where-do-mexicos-1-million-u-s-expats-live/

21 Ibid, Arigoni

Chapter Eight

1 https://www.wola.org/wp-content/uploads/2018/05/ENGL-Corruption-Report.pdf - Great Report on MX - Maureen Meyer is WOLA's Director for Mexico and Migrant Rights. Gina Hinojosa is WOLA's Program Assistant for Mexico - *MEXICO'S NATIONAL ANTI-CORRUPTION SYSTEM A Historic Opportunity in the Fight against Corruption* By: Maureen Meyer and Gina Hinojosa MAY 2018

2 Handy, Charles *The Age of Paradox*, Harvard Business School Press © 1994 p. 221

3 https://mexiconewsdaily.com/news/anti-corruption-plan-sees-little-progress/ - *Anti-Corruption Plan sees Little Progress* - 5/25/2017.

4 Dolan, Matthew The Detroit Free Press, March 5, 2016 *"Flint Water Crisis Could Cost U.S. $300 billion,"* https://www.usatoday.com/story/news/nation-now/2016/03/05/flint-water-crisis-could-cost-us-300-billion/81359834/

5 https://www.pbs.org/wgbh/frontline/article/flint-water-crisis-deaths-likely-surpass-official-toll/

Chapter NINE

1 World Travel & Tourism Council 2017 - Economic Impact Report, Copyright © World Travel & Tourism Council: Travel & Tourism Economic Impact 2017 - March 2017. All rights reserved. https://www.wttc.org/-/media/files/reports/economic-impact-research/regions-2017/world2017.pdf

2 World Travel & Tourism Economic Impact 2018 - Mexico - Economic Impact Report, Copyright © World Travel & Tourism Council: Travel & Tourism Economic Impact 2018 - March 2018. All rights reserved. https://hi-tek.io/assets/tourism-statistics/Mexico2018.pdf

3 UN World Tourism Organization. http://media.unwto.org/en/press-release/2011-10-11/international-tourists-hit-18-billion-2030

4 Williams, A. M. and Baláž, Vallad. *Tourism, Risk and Uncertainty: Theoretical Reflections*, Journal of Travel Research, 54(3): 271 (2015), p. 287

5 Osland , Gregory Mackoy, Robert McCormick, Marleen *Perceptions of personal risk in tourists' destination choices: nature tours in Mexico*, Volume/Issue: Volume 8: Issue 1First Online: 10 Oct 2017 Page Count: 38–50

https://content.sciendo.com/abstract/journals/ejthr/8/1/article-p38.xml

6 Tsaur, Sheng-Hshiung & Tzeng, Gwo-Hshiung & Kuo-Ching, Wang. (1997). *Evaluating tourist risks from fuzzy logic.* Annals of Tourism Research. 24. 7

7 Kozak, Metin and Crotts, John C, and Law, Rob *The impact of the Perception of Risk on International Travelers,* International Journal of Tourism Research, 10 July 2007. Volume 9, Issue 4 July/August 2007 Pages 233-242 Copyright © 2007 John Wiley & Sons, Ltd.

8 SEE:https://travel.state.gov/content/travel/en/traveladvisories/traveladvisories.html/

9 LeClercq, Juan Antonio Eje Central, *Bankruptcy in Public Safety*, October 4, 2018 NOTE: Juan Antonio Le Clercq is Professor of International Relations and Political Science, UDLAP. Director of the Center for Studies on Impunity and Justice, CESIJ. Co-author of the Global Impunity Index. He is also aPh.D., and a nonresident scholar at the Baker Institute Mexico Center and a professor at the University of the Americas Puebla (UDLAP) in Mexico.

10 McDonnell, Patrick J. *Crime Wave, Police Complicity Batter Mexico's Jalisco State and Trigger Angry Protests*, Los Angeles Times March 26, 2018

11 Vincent, Isabel New York Post December 15, 2018 *American Tourists Risk Death to Vacation in Mexico.*

12 Stoller, Gary *Mexico: Where More Americans Are Murdered Than In All Other Foreign Countries Combined,* FORBES February 21, 2018 **NOTE**: This article is based on 2016 statistics and notes: "More than 31 million Americans visited Mexico in 2016, the National Travel & Tourism Office says, and State Department data shows there were reports of 75 American homicide victims there. In comparison, 49 million Americans traveled to all other foreign countries, and 69 were reported killed by homicide."

13 National Travel & Tourism Office:https://travel.trade.gov/outreachpages/outbound.general_information.outbound_overview.asp

14 *7 of the Top Places U.S. Expats Are Living in Latin America (and Why)* https://vivatropical.com/nicaragua/where-expats-live-in-central-america/

15 Garcia, Gabriel *That $30 trillion 'great wealth transfer' is a myth, Gabriel Garcia is managing director and head of relationship management at BNY Mellon's Pershing Advisor Solutions , May 22, 2018.*https://www.cnbc.com/2018/05/22/that-30-trillion-

great-wealth-transfer-is-a-myth.html

16 The Business Year – *Over 6,000 Companies in Jalisco – An Interview with Aristóteles Sandoval Díaz* – Who has governed the western State of Jalisco since 2013. Mexico 2018 | ECONOMY | https://www.thebusinessyear.com/mexico-2018/aristoteles-sandoval-diaz-governor-jalisco/vip-interview

17 *HOW CAN THE CONNECTIVITY IMPACT A TOURIST'S TRAVEL EXPERIENCE THROUGH SOCIAL MEDIA?* December 3, 2015 Brand Base – Brand Management For A Wired World. http://www.brandba.se/blog/2015/12/3/how-can-the-connectivity-impact-a-tourists-travel-experience-through-social-media

18 Peltier, Dan SKIFT *Mexico Tourism Marketing Blitz to Address Safety Concerns After Violence,* May 22, 2018

19 Ibid, Vincent, Isabel

20 US Department of State – Office of Diplomatic Security, *Mexico 2018 Crime & Safety Report: Guadalajara,* https://www.osac.gov/Pages/ContentReportDetails.aspx?cid=23837

Chapter TEN

1 Palfrey, Dale Hoyt The Guadalajara Reporter December 27, 2018 *"Urbanization Plans Multiply on Lake Chapala's Shoreline."* http://theguadalajarareporter.net/index.php/news/news/lake-chapala/52863-urbanization-plans-multiply-on-lake-chapala-s-shoreline

2 Email from Ajijic, MX resident Gary Jones, December 2018.

3 Lake Chapala Reporter article 12-11-2018

4 See Also: Laguna December 10, 2018: *IPEJAL dreams of building a city of 17,000 inhabitants in Chapala:* http://semanariolaguna.com/40237/?fbclid=IwAR3h1OguK7UYqA3-hSNOFJyl3WHuf1NzN7XgpYLhrTSK6CjlK7vBIxlxmE8#.XBB2cRADhlk.facebook

5 Palfrey, Dale Hoyt The Guadalajara Reporter December 27, 2018 *"Urbanization Plans Multiply on Lake Chapala's Shoreline."* http://theguadalajarareporter.net/index.php/news/news/lake-chapala/52863-urbanization-plans-multiply-on-lake-chapala-s-shoreline

6 Ibid, Palfrey quoting Jacobo.

7 SEE: http://www.insidelakeside.com/t20953-follow-up-on-the-hill-development-in-ajijic

8 Translated to English from the group's FB page.

9 January 5, 2019 – Lake Chapala Reporter

10 December 8, 2018 – Lake Chapala Reporter

11 December 13, 2018 – Lake Chapala Reporter

12 December 6, 2018 – Lake Chapala Reporter

13 December 29, 2018 – Lake Chapala Reporter

14 December 6, 2018 – Lake Chapala Reporter

15 December 3, 2018 – Lake Chapala Reporter

16 October 29, 2018 – Lake Chapala Reporter

17 October 26, 2018 – Lake Chapala Reporter

18 November 8, 2018 – Lake Chapala Reporter

19 November 16, 2018 – Lake Chapala Reporter

20 November 22, 2018 – Lake Chapala Reporter

21 Palfrey, Dale Hoyt The Guadalajara Reporter December 27, 2018 *"Urbanization Plans Multiply on Lake Chapala's Shoreline."* http://theguadalajarareporter.net/index.php/news/news/lake-chapala/52863-urbanization-plans-multiply-on-lake-chapala-s-shoreline

Chapter ELEVEN – NO End Notes

Chapter TWELVE

1 http://www.worldometers.info/world-population/mexico-population/

2 Reuters November 2017, *Mexican Congress gives final approval for 2018 budget: https://www.reuters.com/article/us-mexico-budget/mexican-congress-gives-final-approval-for-2018-budget-idUSKBN1DA28I*

3 *Water Pollution Control - A Guide to the Use of Water Quality Management Principles* Edited by Richard Helmer and Ivanildo Hespanhol Published on behalf of the United Nations Environment Programme, the Water Supply & Sanitation Collaborative

Council and the World Health Organization by E. & F. Spon © 1997 WHO/UNEP ISBN 0 419 22910 8 This case study was prepared by José Eduardo Mestre Rodríguez https://www.who.int/water_sanitation_health/resourcesquality/wpccasestudy8.pdf

4 Global Water Intelligence, *Mexican Lower House Doubles Conagua 2019 Budget,* November 22, 2019. https://www.globalwaterintel.com/news/2018/47/mexican-lower-house-doubles-conagua-2019-budget

5 Sánchez-Torres, Juan D .; Nuño-Sánchez, Saúl A .; Martinez-Alvarado, Juan C .; Ruiz-Cruz, Riemann Sánchez-Torres, J.D .; Nuño-Sánchez, S.A .; Martínez-Alvarado, J.C. and Ruiz-Cruz, R. (2018). *Report of Water Quality Data Analysis of Lake Chapala* Department of Mathematics and Physics. Published December 2018. Institute of Technology and Higher Studies of the West: ITESO Tlaquepaque, Jalisco: ITESO. https://rei.iteso.mx/handle/11117/5614

6 Tapia, Omar & López-Caloca, Alejandra. (August 2018). *Calculating long-term changes in Lake Chapala's area and water volume using remote sensing and field data.* Journal of Applied Remote Sensing. 12. 1. 10.1117/1.JRS.12.042805. https://www.researchgate.net/publication/327167877_Calculating_long-term_changes_in_Lake_Chapala's_area_and_water_volume_using_remote_sensing_and_field_data

7 Rodriguez-Sanchez, Jose I. Ph.D., *Measuring Corruption in Mexico*: Postdoctoral Research Fellow in International Trade, Mexico Center - James A. Baker III Institute for Public Policy of Rice University. December 2018. P.4. https://www.bakerinstitute.org/media/files/files/b190ca73/bi-pub-rodriguez-sanchezcorruption-121118.pdf

8 Dimant, Eugen and Tosato, Guglielmo *Causes and Effects of Corruption: What has Past Decade's Empirical Research Taught Us? A Survey.* Available from: [accessed Dec 25 2018].Journal of Economic Surveys (2018) Vol. 32, No. 2, (c) 2017 John Wiley & Sons Ltd.p.351. https://www.researchgate.net/publication/304113926_Causes_and_Effects_of_Corruption_What_has_Past_Decade's_Empirical_Research_Taught_Us_A_Survey

9 Water Integrity Global Outlook 2016 - http://www.waterintegritynetwork.net/wp-content/uploads/delightful-downloads/2016/06/WIGO_2016_ExSummary_EN_final.pdf p.1.

10 Rodriguez-Sanchez, Jose I. Ph.D., *Measuring Corruption in Mexico*: Postdoctoral Research Fellow in International Trade, Mexico Center - James A. Baker III Institute for

Public Policy of Rice University. December 2018. P.14.
https://www.bakerinstitute.org/media/files/files/b190ca73/bi-pub-rodriguez-sanchezcorruption-121118.pdf

11 Rodriguez-Sanchez, Jose I. Ph.D., *Measuring Corruption in Mexico*: Postdoctoral Research Fellow in International Trade, Mexico Center - James A. Baker III Institute for Public Policy of Rice University. December 2018. P.12. **_See also_**: Grajales, Ana Lagunes, Paul Ph.D. Nazal, Tomas "Anatomy of Urban Corruption: A Review of Official Corruption Complaints from a Mexican City" Mexico Center - James A. Baker III Institute for Public Policy of Rice University. Copyright © 2018 by the James A. Baker III Institute for Public Policy of Rice University December 2018. P.4.

12 Grajales, Ana Lagunes, Paul, Ph.D. Nazal , Tomas *"Anatomy of Urban Corruption: A Review of Official Corruption Complaints from a Mexican City"* - © 2018 by the James A. Baker III Institute for Public Policy of Rice University p. 4.
https://www.bakerinstitute.org/media/files/research-document/120a0539/mex-pub-corruption-lagunes-121318.pdf

13 January 2017 - End of mission statement by the United Nations Special Rapporteur on the situation of human rights defenders, Michel Forst on his visit to Mexico from from 16 to 24 January 2017. SEE:
https://www.ohchr.org/EN/NewsEvents/Pages/DisplayNews.aspx?NewsID=21111&LangID=E

14 Global Witness *AT WHAT COST? Irresponsible Business and the Murder of Land and Environmental Defenders in 2017,* A Report by Global Witness / July 24, 2018. SEE: https://www.globalwitness.org/en/campaigns/environmental-activists/at-what-cost/

15 Pickrell , Emily - Bloomberg - Mexico City, SEE:
https://news.bloombergenvironment.com/environment-and-energy/crossing-cartels-leads-to-death-for-mexican-environmentalists

16 del Castillo Negrete, Miguel *Income Inequality in Mexico, 2004–2014,* Latin American Policy, May 2017, Latin American Policy—Volume 8, Number 1—Pages 93–113 © 2017 Policy Studies Organization. Published by Wiley Periodicals, Inc. p.93.

17 Jong-sung, Y., & Khagram, S. (2005). *A Comparative Study of Inequality and Corruption. American Sociological Review, 70* (3), 539–539. https://doi.org/10.1177/000312240507000309

18 Lo, Andrew W. *Adaptive Markets – Financial Evolution at the Speed of Thought,* Copyright © 2017 by Princeton University Press, Princeton, NJ p. 209.

19 Lowenstein, Roger *Origins of the CRASH – The Great Bubble and its Undoing*, Copyright © 2004 by Roger Lowenstein. The Penguin Group, New Copyright © 2004 by Roger Lowenstein. The Penguin Group, New York, NY. P.36.

20 Rothbard, Murray N. *The Panic of 1819 – Reactions and Policies*, Copyright © 1962 Columbia University Press, Ludwig von Mises Institute Auburn, Alabama p. 249.

21 Galbraith, John Kenneth *A History of Economics – The Past as the Present*, Copyright © 1987 by John Kenneth Galbraith, Penguin Books LTD New York, NY and London, UK p. 129.

22 Stolpe, Oliver December 2018 Oliver Stolpe, Country Representative, United Nations Office on Drugs and Crime (UNODC), in Premium Times: https://www.premiumtimesng.com/news/more-news/300215-world-loses-2-3trn-to-corruption-annually-un.html

23 Ibid. Stolpe.

24 Meyer, Maureen and Hinojosa, Gina *MEXICO'S NATIONAL ANTI-CORRUPTION SYSTEM: A Historic Opportunity in the Fight Against Corruption*, MAY 2018 p. 2. https://www.wola.org/wp-content/uploads/2018/05/ENGL-Corruption-Report.pdf

25 December 7, 2018 - People's World:https://www.peoplesworld.org/article/president-andres-manuel-lopez-obrador-promises-new-hope-for-mexicos-future/

26 Rose-Ackerman, Susan and Truex, Rory *Corruption & Policy Reform*, April 2016, P.42. https://www.copenhagenconsensus.com/sites/default/files/workingpaper_corruption. pdf referencing: Olken & Pande (2011)

27 Kaiser, Max Director, Anti-Corruption, IMCO, December 2016, *"This Is How Mexico Is Fighting Corruption,"* https://www.weforum.org/agenda/2016/12/alternative-leadership-in-fighting-corruption-the-mexican-case/

28 Ibid, Kaiser

29 Ibid, Rodriguez-Sanchez, in *Measuring*, p. 10

30 Ibid, Rodriguez-Sanchez, in *Measuring*, p. 11

31 https://knoema.com/atlas/Mexico/GDP

32 Organisation of Economic Cooperation and Development, Mexico Policy Brief –

Environment - IMPROVING CLIMATE ADAPTATION AND WATER MANAGEMENT, January 2017. https://www.oecd.org/policy-briefs/mexico-improving-climate-adaptation-and-water-management.pdf

33 Rose-Ackerman, Susan and Truex, Rory *Corruption & Policy Reform,* April 2016, P.3.https://www.copenhagenconsensus.com/sites/default/files/workingpaper_corruption.pdf

34 Agren, David USA Today November 30, 2018 *Mexico's new president sworn into office, pledges to curb corruption, bring change.* https://www.usatoday.com/story/news/world/2018/11/30/andres-manuel-lopez-obrador-mexico-president-donald-trump-corruption-border-immigration-amlo/1195596002/

35 Rodriguez-Sanchez, Jose I. Ph.D., *Understanding the Problems and Obstacles of Corruption in Mexico*: Postdoctoral Research Fellow in International Trade, Mexico Center, James A. Baker III Institute for Public Policy of Rice University. https://www.bakerinstitute.org/media/files/files/dae461e7/bi-brief-091318-mex-corruption.pdf

36 Barkin, David *Environmental Degradation and Productive Transformation in Mexico: The Contradictions of Crisis Management,* University of Texas Press, *Yearbook (Conference of Latin Americanist Geographers)* Vol. 15 (1989), p. 3.

37 Ibid, Barkin p. 3.

38 Organisation of Economic Cooperation and Development, Mexico Policy Brief – *Environment - IMPROVING CLIMATE ADAPTATION AND WATER MANAGEMENT,* January 2017. https://www.oecd.org/policy-briefs/mexico-improving-climate-adaptation-and-water-management.pdf

39 Slater, Philip *The Pursuit of Loneliness,* Beacon Press Boston, MA Copyright © 1970 & 1976 by Philip E. Slater. P. 19.

40 Ibid. Slater, p. xii.

41 Dahl, Bill & Vazquez-Sanchez, Gabriel, *NaturAMLO – The Amazing Mexico Leadership Opportunity – The Amelioration Mandate for Lake Chapala's Oversight,* December 2018. © 2018 Bill Dahl

42 Dahl, Bill *Mexi-CUTE or Mexi-CURE: Lake Chapala is a Sick Puppy - The Opportunity for President Lopez-Obrador in The Lake Chapala Basin,* © 2018 by Bill Dahl: https://www.billdahl.net/articles/mexi-cute-or-mexi-cure-lake-chapala-is-a-sick-puppy/

43 del Castillo Negrete, Miguel *Income Inequality in Mexico, 2004–2014,* May 2017, Latin American Policy—Volume 8, Number 1—Pages 93–113 © 2017 Policy Studies Organization. Published by Wiley Periodicals, Inc. p.111.

44 Dupuy, Kendra and Neset, Siri *The cognitive psychology of corruption -Micro-level explanations for unethical behaviour,* U4 Anti-Corruption Resource Centre, Chr. Michelsen Institute (U4 Issue 2018:2) p.2.

45 Kaufman, Daniel *Rethinking The Fight Against Corruption,* Bookings Institute, November 2012.

46 Heywood, Paul M. *Combating Corruption in the Twenty-First Century: New Approaches*: https://core.ac.uk/download/pdf/151445634.pdf Paul M. Heywood is the Sir Francis Hill Professor of European Politics in the School of Politics and International Relations at the University of Nottingham. He is the author of Political Corruption (1997) and The Government and Politics of Spain (1995) and editor of the Routledge Handbook of Political Corruption (2015). P.2.

47 Cherry, Kendra *The Basics of Cognition,* November 2018, VeryWellMind: https://www.verywellmind.com/what-is-cognition-2794982

48 Gottschall, Jonathan *The Storytelling Animal - How Stories Make Us Human.* Houghton Mifflin Harcourt Publishing Company New York, NY Copyright (c) 2012 by Jonathan Gottschall, pp. xiv and xvii.

49 Harari, Yuvall Noah *Homo Deus – A Brief History of Tomorrow,* Harper – An Imprint of HarperCollinsPublishers New York, NY Copyright © 2017 by Yuvall Noah Harari p. 156.

50 Dahl, Bill *KNOWMENTARY – A New Term from Bill Dahl,* August 2012, *https://www.billdahl.net/articles/knowmentary-a-new-word-from-bill-dahl/*

51 Dupuy, Kendra and Neset, Siri *The cognitive psychology of corruption -Micro-level explanations for unethical behaviour,* U4 Anti-Corruption Resource Centre, Chr. Michelsen Institute (U4 Issue 2018:2): See section: *Rational choice-inspired anti-corruption policy has failed.* https://www.u4.no/publications/the-cognitive-psychology-of-corruption

52 Kahneman, Daniel. *Thinking, Fast and Slow.* New York: Farrar, Straus and Giroux, 2011.p. 45.

53 Shermer, Michael *The Believing Brain - From Ghosts and Gods to Politics and Conspiracies - How we construct Beliefs and Reinforce Them As Truths,* St. Martin's

Griffin - St. Martin's Press New York, NY Copyright (c) 2011 by Michael Shermer. P. 453.

54 Driver, Janine with Van Aalst, Mariska *You Can't Lie To Me,* HarperOne - An Imprint of HarperCollinsPublishers *New York, NY* Copyright (c) 2012 by Janine Driver. P. 35.

55 Shermer, Michael *The Believing Brain - From Ghosts and Gods to Politics and Conspiracies - How we construct Beliefs and Reinforce Them As Truths*, St. Martin's Griffin - St. Martin's Press New York, NY Copyright (c) 2011 by Michael Shermer. P. 344.

56 Dahl, Bill & Vazquez-Sanchez, Gabriel, *NaturAMLO – The Amazing Mexico Leadership Opportunity – The Amelioration Mandate for Lake Chapala's Oversight,* December 2018. © 2018 Bill Dahl

57 Trivers, Robert *The Folly of Fools – The Logic of Deceit and Self-Deception in Human Life,* Basic Books – A Division of the Perseus Books Group New York, NY Copyright © 2011 by Robert Trivers p. 338 & 336.

58 Driver, Janine with Van Aalst, Mariska *You Can't Lie To Me,* HarperOne - An Imprint of HarperCollinsPublishers *New York, NY* Copyright (c) 2012 by Janine Driver p. 39.

59 Dahl, Bill *Mexiconsiderations – Lake Chapala and The Fifth Risk,* © 2018 by Bill Dahl,https://www.billdahl.net/articles/mexiconsiderations-lake-chapala-and-the-fifth-risk/

60 Baillat Aline, 2013; *Corruption and the Human Right to Water and Sanitation-Human right-based Approach to Tackling Corruption in the Water Sector*; WaterLex, Geneva and Water Integrity Network, Berlin © 2013 WaterLex and Water Integrity Network (WIN): https://www.waterlex.org/new/wp-content/uploads/2013/12/2013-WaterLex-WIN_Corruption-and-the-HRWS-.pdf p. 6.

61 Baillat Aline, 2013; Corruption and the human right to water and sanitation-Human right-based approach to tackling corruption in the water sector; WaterLex, Geneva and Water Integrity Network, Berlin © 2013 WaterLex and Water Integrity Network (WIN): https://www.waterlex.org/new/wp-content/uploads/2013/12/2013-WaterLex-WIN_Corruption-and-the-HRWS-.pdf p.10.

62 Rose-Ackerman, Susan *Corruption & Purity*, Susan Rose-Ackerman is the Henry R. Luce Professor of Jurisprudence (Law and Political Science) Yale University.https://www.nhh.no/globalassets/departments/accounting-auditing-and-

law/seminar-papers/daedalus_rose-ackerman_clean_3.30.18.pdf p. 1.

63 Rose-Ackerman, Susan *Corruption & Purity*, Susan Rose-Ackerman is the Henry R. Luce Professor of Jurisprudence (Law and Political Science) Yale University.https://www.nhh.no/globalassets/departments/accounting-auditing-and-law/seminar-papers/daedalus_rose-ackerman_clean_3.30.18.pdf p. 3.

64 Grajales, Ana Lagunes, Paul, Ph.D. Nazal , Tomas *"Anatomy of Urban Corruption: A Review of Official Corruption Complaints from a Mexican City"* - © 2018 by the James A. Baker III Institute for Public Policy of Rice University p. 1. https://www.bakerinstitute.org/media/files/research-document/120a0539/mex-pub-corruption-lagunes-121318.pdf

65 Kaufman, Daniel *Rethinking The Fight Against Corruption*, Bookings Institute, November 2012.

66 **NOTE:** Excerpt from: https://www.bakerinstitute.org/experts/jose-ivan-rodriguezsanchez/

Jose Ivan Rodriguez-Sanchez, Ph.D., is the postdoctoral research fellow in international trade for the Baker Institute Mexico Center. His research focuses on international trade, migration, environmental economics and economic growth. Prior to joining the Baker Institute, he studied the energy and water markets of the Paso del Norte region as a research associate for the Hunt Institute at The University of Texas at El Paso. Rodriguez-Sanchez also worked as a deputy director in environmental economics at the Instituto Nacional de Ecología y Cambio Climático (INECC), where he analyzed different environmental problems in Mexico and crafted different public policy solutions. He has taught economics classes and seminars at the University of Colorado at Boulder, Instituto Tecnológico y de Estudios Superiores de Monterrey, Universidad Iberoamericana Puebla, Universidad de las Américas Puebla, Universidad Popular Autónoma del Estado de Puebla and Universidad Tecnológica de la Mixteca. His work has also been published in both academic and non-academic publications.

Rodriguez-Sanchez received a bachelor's degree in actuarial science and a master's degree in economics from the Universidad de las Américas Puebla, and master's and doctoral degrees in economics from the University of Colorado at Boulder, where he specialized in environmental economics, international trade and econometrics.

67 Rodriguez-Sanchez, Jose I. Ph.D., *Measuring Corruption in Mexico*: Postdoctoral Research Fellow in International Trade, Mexico Center - James A. Baker III Institute for Public Policy of Rice University. December 2018. P.14. https://www.bakerinstitute.org/media/files/files/b190ca73/bi-pub-rodriguez-

sanchezcorruption-121118.pdf

68 https://www.pbs.org/wgbh/frontline/article/flint-water-crisis-deaths-likely-surpass-official-toll/

69 https://www.mlive.com/news/flint/index.ssf/2018/05/heres_whats_next_for_11_defend.html

70 See: https://www.greghillassociates.com/what-is-involuntary-manslaughter-defenses-punishment.html

71 Dolan, Matthew The Detroit Free Press, March 5, 2016 *"Flint Water Crisis Could Cost U.S. $300 billion,"* https://www.usatoday.com/story/news/nation-now/2016/03/05/flint-water-crisis-could-cost-us-300-billion/81359834/

72 Ibid, PBS Note #1

73 For avian species contamination, see this source as a starting point. Excerpt From: https://www.researchgate.net/publication/324904635_Biomonitoreo_de_metal es_pesados_en_plumas_de_aves_acuaticas_residentes_del_Lago_de_Chapala_Mexic o The resident waterfowl of Lake Chapala,A. alba , E. thula and N. nycticorax , proved to be good indicators of metal pollution heavy, which were found in concentrations high in the feathers of the three species. (PDF Available) *in* International Journal of Environmental Contamination 34 (2): 215-224 · May 2018

74 For Chronic Kidney Disease, SEE: Garcia-Garcia, Guillermo and Chavez-Iniguez, Jonathan Samuel *The Tragedy of Having ESRD in Mexico*, Kidney International Reports, 2018 Sep; 3(5): 1027–1029.

75 Sánchez-Torres, Juan D .; Nuño-Sánchez, Saúl A .; Martinez-Alvarado, Juan C .; Ruiz-Cruz, Riemann Sánchez-Torres, J.D .; Nuño-Sánchez, S.A .; Martínez-Alvarado, J.C. and Ruiz-Cruz, R. (2018). *Report of Water Quality Data Analysis of Lake Chapala* Department of Mathematics and Physics. Published December 2018. Institute of Technology and Higher Studies of the West: ITESO Tlaquepaque, Jalisco: ITESO. https://rei.iteso.mx/handle/11117/5614

76 Bhargava, Dr. Vinay Director, International Affairs, The World Bank, *The Cancer of Corruption*, World Bank Global Issues Seminar Series, p. 3.

77 Organisation of Economic Cooperation and Development, Mexico Policy Brief – *Environment - IMPROVING CLIMATE ADAPTATION AND WATER MANAGEMENT*, January 2017. https://www.oecd.org/policy-briefs/mexico-improving-climate-adaptation-and-water-management.pdf

78 Kaiser, Max Director, Anti-Corruption, IMCO, December 2016, *"This Is How Mexico Is Fighting Corruption,"* https://www.weforum.org/agenda/2016/12/alternative-leadership-in-fighting-corruption-the-mexican-case/

79 Ibid, PBS Note #1

80 Rodriguez-Sanchez, Jose I. Ph.D., *Understanding the Problems and Obstacles of Corruption in Mexico*: Postdoctoral Research Fellow in International Trade, Mexico Center – Baker Center https://www.bakerinstitute.org/media/files/files/dae461e7/bi-brief-091318-mex-corruption.pdf p. 2.

81 See: https://www.cnbc.com/2018/11/23/china-steps-up-prosecutions-for-pollution-offences.html

82 Transcript of the Latin American Water Council Court Hearings in October 2018 on the environmental and public health hazards resident in the Lerma-Chapala basin in Mexico were provided to the author by Gabriel Vazquez-Sanchez - the General Director of AIROMADES – the Intermunicipal Association for the Protection of the Environment and Sustainable Development of Lake Chapala. The full English text can be found HERE: https://www.billdahl.net/articles/lake-chapala-verdict-of-the-court-of-the-latin-american-water-tribunal-october-2018/

83 Ibid, above.

84 SEE: https://www.ey.com/Publication/vwLUAssets/ey-white-paper-mexico-colombia-anti-bribery-laws/$FILE/ey-white-paper-mexico-colombia-anti-bribery-laws.pdf

85 Meyer, Maureen and Hinojosa, Gina *MEXICO'S NATIONAL ANTI-CORRUPTION SYSTEM: A Historic Opportunity in the Fight Against Corruption,* MAY 2018 p. 2. https://www.wola.org/wp-content/uploads/2018/05/ENGL-Corruption-Report.pdf

86 *Anti-Corruption Plan sees Little Progress* - 5/25/2017: SEE:https://mexiconewsdaily.com/news/anti-corruption-plan-sees-little-progress/

87 Rodriguez-Sanchez, Jose I. Ph.D., *Measuring Corruption in Mexico*: Postdoctoral Research Fellow in International Trade, Mexico Center - James A. Baker III Institute for Public Policy of Rice University. December 2018. P. 15. https://www.bakerinstitute.org/media/files/files/b190ca73/bi-pub-rodriguez-sanchezcorruption-121118.pdf

88 Global Water Intelligence, *Mexican Lower House Doubles Conagua 2019 Budget,* November 22, 2018. https://www.globalwaterintel.com/news/2018/47/mexican-lower-

house-doubles-conagua-2019-budget

89 Organisation of Economic Cooperation and Development, Mexico Policy Brief – *Environment - IMPROVING CLIMATE ADAPTATION AND WATER MANAGEMENT*, January 2017. https://www.oecd.org/policy-briefs/mexico-improving-climate-adaptation-and-water-management.pdf

90 Heywood, Paul M. *Combating Corruption in the Twenty-First Century: New Approaches*: https://core.ac.uk/download/pdf/151445634.pdf Paul M. Heywood is the Sir Francis Hill Professor of European Politics in the School of Politics and International Relations at the University of Nottingham. He is the author of Political Corruption (1997) and The Government and Politics of Spain (1995) and editor of the Routledge Handbook of Political Corruption (2015). P. 19.

91 For more information of water hyacinths as an invasive species, SEE: Villamagna, Amy & Murphy, Brian. (2008). *Water Resources Management in the Lerma–Chapala Basin, Mexico: A Case Study*. Journal of Natural Resources and Life Sciences Education. 37. 102-110. 10.2134/jnrlse2008.371102x. https://www.researchgate.net/publication/251566510_Water_Resources_Management_in_the_Lerma-Chapala_Basin_Mexico_A_Case_Study

92 Heywood, Paul M. *Combating Corruption in the Twenty-First Century: New Approaches*: https://core.ac.uk/download/pdf/151445634.pdf Paul M. Heywood is the Sir Francis Hill Professor of European Politics in the School of Politics and International Relations at the University of Nottingham. He is the author of Political Corruption (1997) and The Government and Politics of Spain (1995) and editor of the Routledge Handbook of Political Corruption (2015). P. 19.

ALPHABETICAL ENDNOTES CHAPTER TWELVE

Corruption in Mexico: An Environmental and Public Health Perspective by Bill Dahl © 2019

Agren, David USA Today November 30, 2018 *Mexico's new president sworn into office, pledges to curb corruption, bring change.* https://www.usatoday.com/story/news/world/2018/11/30/andres-manuel-lopez-obrador-mexico-president-donald-trump-corruption-border-immigration-amlo/1195596002/ (34)

Baillat, Aline 2013; *Corruption and the Human Right to Water and Sanitation-*

Human right-based Approach to Tackling Corruption in the Water Sector; WaterLex, Geneva and Water Integrity Network, Berlin © 2013 WaterLex and Water Integrity Network (WIN): https://www.waterlex.org/new/wp-content/uploads/2013/12/2013-WaterLex-WIN_Corruption-and-the-HRWS-.pdf p. 6. (60)

Barkin, David *Environmental Degradation and Productive Transformation in Mexico: The Contradictions of Crisis Management,* University of Texas Press, *Yearbook (Conference of Latin Americanist Geographers)* Vol. 15 (1989), p. 3. (36)

Bhargava, Dr. Vinay Director, International Affairs, The World Bank, *The Cancer of Corruption*, World Bank Global Issues Seminar Series, p. 3. (73)

Cherry, Kendra *The Basics of Cognition,* November 2018, VeryWellMind: https://www.verywellmind.com/what-is-cognition-2794982 (47)

del Castillo Negrete, Miguel *Income Inequality in Mexico, 2004–2014,* Latin American Policy, May 2017, Latin American Policy—Volume 8, Number 1—Pages 93–113 © 2017 Policy Studies Organization. Published by Wiley Periodicals, Inc. p.93. (16)

Dahl, Bill *KNOWMENTARY – A New Term from Bill Dahl,* August 2012, *https://www.billdahl.net/articles/knowmentary-a-new-word-from-bill-dahl/* (50)

Dahl, Bill & Vazquez-Sanchez, Gabriel, *NaturAMLO – The Amazing Mexico Leadership Opportunity – The Amelioration Mandate for Lake Chapala's Oversight,* December 2018. © 2018 Bill Dahl (41)

Dahl, Bill *Mexiconsiderations – Lake Chapala and The Fifth Risk,* © 2018 by Bill Dahl,https://www.billdahl.net/articles/mexiconsiderations-lake-chapala-and-the-fifth-risk/ (59)

Dahl, Bill *Mexi-CUTE or Mexi-CURE: Lake Chapala is a Sick Puppy - The Opportunity for President Lopez-Obrador in The Lake Chapala Basin,* © 2018 by Bill Dahl: https://www.billdahl.net/articles/mexi-cute-or-mexi-cure-lake-chapala-is-a-sick-puppy/ (42)

Dimant, Eugen and Tosato, Guglielmo *Causes and Effects of Corruption: What has Past Decade's Empirical Research Taught Us? A Survey.* Available from: [accessed Dec 25 2018].Journal of Economic Surveys (2018) Vol. 32, No. 2, (c) 2017 John Wiley & Sons Ltd.p.351.
https://www.researchgate.net/publication/304113926_Causes_and_Effects_of_Corruption_What_has_Past_Decade's_Empirical_Research_Taught_Us_A_Survey (8)

Dolan, Matthew The Detroit Free Press, March 5, 2016 *"Flint Water Crisis Could Cost*

U.S. $300 billion," https://www.usatoday.com/story/news/nation-now/2016/03/05/flint-water-crisis-could-cost-us-300-billion/81359834/ (70)

Driver, Janine with Van Aalst, Mariska *You Can't Lie To Me,* HarperOne - An Imprint of HarperCollinsPublishers *New York, NY* Copyright (c) 2012 by Janine Driver. P. 35. (54)

Dupuy, Kendra and Neset, Siri *The cognitive psychology of corruption -Micro-level explanations for unethical behaviour,* U4 Anti-Corruption Resource Centre, Chr. Michelsen Institute (U4 Issue 2018:2) p.2.(44)

Galbraith, John Kenneth *A History of Economics – The Past as the Present,* Copyright © 1987 by John Kenneth Galbraith, Penguin Books LTD New York, NY and London, UK p. 129. (21)

Garcia-Garcia, Guillermo and Chavez-Iniguez, Jonathan Samuel *The Tragedy of Having ESRD in Mexico,* Kidney International Reports, 2018 Sep; 3(5): 1027–1029.

Global Water Intelligence, *Mexican Lower House Doubles Conagua 2019 Budget,* November 22, 2019. https://www.globalwaterintel.com/news/2018/47/mexican-lower-house-doubles-conagua-2019-budget (4)

Global Witness *AT WHAT COST? Irresponsible Business and the Murder of Land and Environmental Defenders in 2017,* A Report by Global Witness / July 24, 2018. SEE: https://www.globalwitness.org/en/campaigns/environmental-activists/at-what-cost/ (14)

Gottschall, Jonathan *The Storytelling Animal - How Stories Make Us Human.* Houghton Mifflin Harcourt Publishing Company New York, NY Copyright (c) 2012 by Jonathan Gottschall, pp. xiv and xvii. (48)

Grajales, Ana Lagunes, Paul, Ph.D. Nazal , Tomas *"Anatomy of Urban Corruption: A Review of Official Corruption Complaints from a Mexican City"* - © 2018 by the James A. Baker III Institute for Public Policy of Rice University p. 4. https://www.bakerinstitute.org/media/files/research-document/120a0539/mex-pub-corruption-lagunes-121318.pdf (12)

Harari, Yuvall Noah *Homo Deus – A Brief History of Tomorrow,* Harper – An Imprint of HarperCollinsPublishers New York, NY Copyright © 2017 by Yuvall Noah Harari p. 156. (49)

Heywood, Paul M. *Combating Corruption in the Twenty-First Century: New Approaches*: https://core.ac.uk/download/pdf/151445634.pdf Paul M. Heywood is the Sir Francis Hill Professor of European Politics in the School of Politics and International

Relations at the University of Nottingham. He is the author of Political Corruption (1997) and The Government and Politics of Spain (1995) and editor of the Routledge Handbook of Political Corruption (2015). P 2 (46)

Hill, Greg & Associates: See: https://www.greghillassociates.com/what-is-involuntary-manslaughter-defenses-punishment.html (69)

Jong-sung, Y., & Khagram, S. (2005). *A Comparative Study of Inequality and Corruption. American Sociological Review, 70* (3), 539–539. https://doi.org/10.1177/000312240507000309 (17)

Kahneman, Daniel. *Thinking, Fast and Slow*. New York: Farrar, Straus and Giroux, 2011.p. 45. (52)

Kaiser, Max Director, Anti-Corruption, IMCO, December 2016, *"This Is How Mexico Is Fighting Corruption,"* https://www.weforum.org/agenda/2016/12/alternative-leadership-in-fighting-corruption-the-mexican-case/(27)

Kaufman, Daniel *Rethinking The Fight Against Corruption*, Bookings Institute, November 2012. (45)

Latin American Water Council Transcript of the Court Hearings in October 2018 on the environmental and public health hazards resident in the Lerma-Chapala basin in Mexico were provided to the author by Gabriel Vazquez-Sanchez - the General Director of AIROMADES – the Intermunicipal Association for the Protection of the Environment and Sustainable Development of Lake Chapala. The full English text can be found HERE: https://www.billdahl.net/articles/lake-chapala-verdict-of-the-court-of-the-latin-american-water-tribunal-october-2018/ (79)

Lo, Andrew W. *Adaptive Markets – Financial Evolution at the Speed of Thought*, Copyright © 2017 by Princeton University Press, Princeton, NJ p. 209.(18)

Lowenstein, Roger *Origins of the CRASH – The Great Bubble and its Undoing*, Copyright © 2004 by Roger Lowenstein. The Penguin Group, New Copyright © 2004 by Roger Lowenstein. The Penguin Group, New York, NY. P.36. (19)

Mestre, Jose Eduardo - *Water Pollution Control - A Guide to the Use of Water Quality Management Principles* Edited by Richard Helmer and Ivanildo Hespanhol Published on behalf of the United Nations Environment Programme, the Water Supply & Sanitation Collaborative Council and the World Health Organization by E. & F. Spon © 1997 WHO/UNEP ISBN 0 419 22910 8 This case study was prepared by José Eduardo Mestre

Rodríguez   https://www.who.int/water_sanitation_health/resourcesquality/wpccasest
udy8.pdf (3)

Mexico Daily News - *Anti-Corruption Plan sees Little Progress* - 5/25/2017:
SEE:https://mexiconewsdaily.com/news/anti-corruption-plan-sees-little-
progress/ (83)

Meyer, Maureen and Hinojosa, Gina *MEXICO'S NATIONAL ANTI-CORRUPTION
SYSTEM: A Historic Opportunity in the Fight Against Corruption,* MAY 2018 p. 2.
https://www.wola.org/wp-content/uploads/2018/05/ENGL-Corruption-
Report.pdf (24)

OECD - Organisation of Economic Cooperation and Development, Mexico Policy Brief
– *Environment - IMPROVING CLIMATE ADAPTATION AND WATER
MANAGEMENT,* January 2017. https://www.oecd.org/policy-briefs/mexico-
improving-climate-adaptation-and-water-management.pdf (32)

PBS: https://www.pbs.org/wgbh/frontline/article/flint-water-crisis-deaths-likely-
surpass-official-toll/ (67)

People's World December 7, 2018 - People's
World:https://www.peoplesworld.org/article/president-andres-manuel-lopez-obrador-
promises-new-hope-for-mexicos-future/ (25)

Pickrell , Emily - Bloomberg - Mexico City, SEE:
https://news.bloombergenvironment.com/environment-and-energy/crossing-cartels-
leads-to-death-for-mexican-environmentalists (15)

Reuters November 2017, *Mexican Congress Gives Final Approval for 2018 Budget:
https://www.reuters.com/article/us-mexico-budget/mexican-congress-gives-final-
approval-for-2018-budget-idUSKBN1DA28I* (2)

Rodriguez-Sanchez, Jose I. Ph.D., *Measuring Corruption in Mexico*: Postdoctoral
Research Fellow in International Trade, Mexico Center - James A. Baker III Institute for
Public Policy of Rice University. December 2018. P.4.
https://www.bakerinstitute.org/media/files/files/b190ca73/bi-pub-rodriguez-
sanchezcorruption-121118.pdf (7 & others)

Rodriguez-Sanchez, Jose I. Ph.D., *Understanding the Problems and Obstacles of
Corruption in Mexico*: Postdoctoral Research Fellow in International Trade, Mexico
Center, James A. Baker III Institute for Public Policy of Rice University.
https://www.bakerinstitute.org/media/files/files/dae461e7/bi-brief-091318-mex-
corruption.pdf (35)

Rose-Ackerman, Susan and Truex, Rory *Corruption & Policy Reform,* April 2016, P.42. https://www.copenhagenconsensus.com/sites/default/files/workingpaper_corruption. pdf referencing: Olken & Pande (2011) (26)

Rose-Ackerman, Susan *Corruption & Purity*, Susan Rose-Ackerman is the Henry R. Luce Professor of Jurisprudence (Law and Political Science) Yale University.https://www.nhh.no/globalassets/departments/accounting-auditing-and-law/seminar-papers/daedalus_rose-ackerman_clean_3.30.18.pdf p. 1. (61)

Rothbard, Murray N. *The Panic of 1819 – Reactions and Policies,* Copyright © 1962 Columbia University Press, Ludwig von Mises Institute Auburn, Alabama p. 249. (20)

Sánchez-Torres, Juan D.; Nuño-Sánchez, Saúl A .; Martinez-Alvarado, Juan C .; Ruiz-Cruz, Riemann Sánchez-Torres, J.D .; Nuño-Sánchez, S.A .; Martínez-Alvarado, J.C. and Ruiz-Cruz, R. (2018). *Report of Water Quality Data Analysis of Lake Chapala* Department of Mathematics and Physics. Published December 2018. Institute of Technology and Higher Studies of the West: ITESO Tlaquepaque, Jalisco: ITESO. https://rei.iteso.mx/handle/11117/5614 (5)

Shermer, Michael *The Believing Brain - From Ghosts and Gods to Politics and Conspiracies - How we construct Beliefs and Reinforce Them As Truths*, St. Martin's Griffin - St. Martin's Press New York, NY Copyright (c) 2011 by Michael Shermer. P. 453. (53)

Slater, Philip *The Pursuit of Loneliness,* Beacon Press Boston, MA Copyright © 1970 & 1976 by Philip E. Slater. P. 19. (39)

Tapia, Omar & López-Caloca, Alejandra. (August 2018). *Calculating long-term changes in Lake Chapala's area and water volume using remote sensing and field data.* Journal of Applied Remote Sensing. 12. 1. 10.1117/1.JRS.12.042805. https://www.researchgate.net/publication/327167877_Calculating_long-term_changes_in_Lake_Chapala's_area_and_water_volume_using_remote_sensing_and_field_data (6)

Trivers, Robert *The Folly of Fools – The Logic of Deceit and Self-Deception in Human Life,* Basic Books – A Division of the Perseus Books Group New York, NY Copyright © 2011 by Robert Trivers p. 338 & 336. (57)

United Nations - January 2017 - End of mission statement by the United Nations Special Rapporteur on the situation of human rights defenders, Michel Forst on his visit to Mexico from from 16 to 24 January 2017. SEE:

https://www.ohchr.org/EN/NewsEvents/Pages/DisplayNews.aspx?NewsID=21111&LangID=E (13)

United Nations Stolpe, Oliver December 2018 Oliver Stolpe, Country Representative, United Nations Office on Drugs and Crime (UNODC), in Premium Times: https://www.premiumtimesng.com/news/more-news/300215-world-loses-2-3trn-to-corruption-annually-un.html (22)

Villamagna, Amy & Murphy, Brian. (2008). *Water Resources Management in the Lerma–Chapala Basin, Mexico: A Case Study*. Journal of Natural Resources and Life Sciences Education. 37. 102-110. 10.2134/jnrlse2008.371102x. (88).

Water Integrity Global Outlook 2016 - http://www.waterintegritynetwork.net/wp-content/uploads/delightful-downloads/2016/06/WIGO_2016_ExSummary_EN_final.pdf p.1. (9)

The **World Bank**, Bhargava, Dr. Vinay Director, International Affairs, The World Bank, *The Cancer of Corruption*, World Bank Global Issues Seminar Series, p. 3. (73)

Worldometers http://www.worldometers.info/world-population/mexico-population/ (1)

EPILOGUE Notes

1 Patel, Eboo Patel, Eboo – *Acts of Faith – The Story of an American Muslim - The Struggle for the Soul of a Generation*, Beacon Press, Boston, MA Copyright © 2007 by Eboo Patel.p. 180.

NOTES – A Cautionary Note

2 Freedom of the Press 2017, Press Freedom's Dark Horizon, https://freedomhouse.org/report/freedom-press/freedom-press-2017

3 Skerlos, Quinn *Violence Against The Press in Mexico*, August 27, 2018, https://justiceinmexico.org/author/lclementlarosa/

4 https://rsf.org/en/ranking